Going Over to Your Place

Going Over to Your Place

POEMS FOR EACH OTHER

Selected by Paul B. Janeczko

Bradbury Press · New York

Bradbury Press
An Affiliate of Macmillan, Inc.
866 Third Avenue, New York, NY 10022
Collier Macmillan Canada, Inc.
Manufactured in the United States of America
10 9 8 7 6 5 4 3 2 1
The text of this book is set in 14 pt. Goudy Old Style.

Library of Congress Cataloging-in-Publication Data
Going over to your place.
Summary: Over 100 poems reflect the rich and varied
experiences of life, from music lessons and a circus
parade to a first kiss and other affairs of the heart.
1. American poetry—20th century. 2. English
poetry—20th century. [1. American poetry—Collections.
2. English poetry—Collections] I. Janeczko, Paul B.
PS615.G59 1987 811'.54'08 86-26439
ISBN 0-02-747670-7

For Kim Mathews and Peter Vose,
the other Beards,
in admiration and friendship

The Heart's Location, *Peter Meinke* 1

&ᴖ **Part One**

Storm Warnings, *Adrienne Rich* 5

Spring Storm, *Jim Wayne Miller* 6
One-Night Fair, *Nancy Price* 6
Into Fish, *Sheryl L. Nelms* 7

while dissecting frogs . . . , *George Roberts* 9
Between You and Me, *Samuel Hazo* 9
Kidnap Poem, *Nikki Giovanni* 10
First Kiss, *Jonathan Holden* 11
First Love, *Stanley Kunitz* 12
The Sound of Rain, *David Allan Evans* 12

At the St. Louis Institute of Music, *Ronald Wallace* 14
Whitley at Three O'Clock, *Jeff Worley* 15
Empty Holds a Question, *Pat Folk* 17

Poet in Residence at a Country School, *Don Welch* 18
What the Stone Dreams, *James B. Hathaway* 19
He Sits Down on the Floor of a School
    for the Retarded, *Alden Nowlan* 20
To a Blind Student Who Taught Me to See, *Samuel Hazo* 22

Myrtle, *Ted Kooser* 24
For Wilma, *Don Johnson* 24
On Being Much Better Than Most and Yet Not Quite Good
    Enough, *John Ciardi* 26
The Man Who Owned Cars, *Elliot Fried* 26
Laughing Backwards, *Jim Hall* 29

Part Two

Living with Children, *Jim Wayne Miller*   33

First Song, *Galway Kinnell*   34
Passage, *John M. Roderick*   34
The Biplane, *Steve Orlen*   36

To My Daughter Riding in the Circus Parade, *Joan
     LaBombard*   38
To a Sad Daughter, *Michael Ondaatje*   39
Departing Words to a Son, *Robert Pack*   42
Father to Son, *Elizabeth Jennings*   44
A Child's Grave Marker, *Ted Kooser*   45

Lament, *George Roberts*   46
Abraham, *George Bogin*   46
For My Brother Who Died Before I Was Born, *Baron
     Wormser*   47

A Man of Action, *Charles B. Stetler*   49
Arm Wrestling with My Father, *Jack Driscoll*   49
A Testimony, *George Ella Lyon*   50
Stopping by Home, *David Huddle*   51
Tunes for Bears to Dance To, *Ronald Wallace*   57
A Daughter's House, *Norma Hope Richman*   58

Manners, *Elizabeth Bishop*   60
Shooting Crows, *David Huddle*   61
My Grandfather in Search of Moonshine, *George Ella
     Lyon*   62

Grandmother Grace, *Ronald Wallace*   64
Days through Starch and Bluing, *Alice Fulton*   65
Grandma Chooses Her Plot at the County Cemetery, *Paul
     Ruffin*   67

Moving, *Frank Steele*   68
Note to the Previous Tenants, *John Updike*   69
The New House, *Vern Rutsala*   70

Late, Passing Prairie Farm, *William Stafford*   72
Incident, *Karl Kopp*   73

You Came as a Thought, *J. Laughlin*   74
Sketch, *Robert Farnsworth*   74
The Meeting, *Howard Moss*   75

Waking, the Love Poem Sighs, *Jim Hall*   77
Rechargeable Dry Cell Poem, *Jim Wayne Miller*   78
My Love, *Richard Shelton*   78
Warmth, *Barton Sutter*   79

Scaffolding, *Seamus Heaney*   80
The Anniversary, *William Dickey*   80

Past Love, *Anne Keiter*   82
A Visit from Alphonse, *Paul Zimmer*   82
Brief Encounter, *Winfield Townley Scott*   83
He Runs into an Old Acquaintance, *Alden Nowlan*   84
The Sunday News, *Dana Gioia*   85
For Her, *Mark Strand*   86
Everything We Do, *Peter Meinke*   87
Sweetheart, *Phil Hey*   88
One Rose of Stone, *Keith Wilson*   88

🌿 Part Three

Quilt Song, *Mark Vinz*   91

Since You Seem Intent . . ., *Gerald Locklin*   92
The Departure, *Frank Steele*   93

This Love, *Judith Hemschemeyer*   93
September: Last Day at the Beach, *Richard Tillinghast*   94
The Goodbye, *Myra Sklarew*   95
First, Goodbye, *John Smith*   96

Absence, *Elizabeth Knies*   98
Dido's Farewell, *Linda Pastan*   93
Thinking of Love, *Elizabeth Jennings*   99

For a Friend, *Ted Kooser*   100
X, Oh X, *Mark Simpson*   101
Beaver Moon—The Suicide of a Friend, *Mary Oliver*   101

Moonlight, *Sara Teasdale*   103
Warning, *Jenny Joseph*   103
Hardy Perennial, *Richard Eberhart*   104
I Dreamed That I Was Old, *Stanley Kunitz*   105
Ago, *Elizabeth Jennings*   106
Blue Springs, Georgia, *Ree Young*   106

The Belly Dancer in the Nursing Home, *Ronald Wallace*   108
Jane Seagrim's Party, *Leonard Nathan*   109

In the Basement of the Goodwill Store, *Ted Kooser*   110
Old Clothes, *Phil Hey*   111

Song for a Departure, *Elizabeth Jennings*   112
Call Them Back, *Chris Petrakos*   113

Return, *Mark Vinz*   114
Looking Both Ways, *Jane O. Wayne*   114
A Prayer for Rivers, *Keith Wilson*   115
Great Things Have Happened, *Alden Nowlan*   116
Some Night Again, *William Stafford*   117

Tomorrow, *Mark Strand*   118
Waiting, *Robert Pack*   118

Part Four

Julian Barely Misses Zimmer's Brains, *Paul Zimmer* 123

A Story That Could Be True, *William Stafford* 124
Suburban, *H. R. Coursen* 124

Reading Room, the New York Public Library, *Richard
    Eberhart* 126
The Lost Carnival, *Fred Chappell* 127
On Certain Mornings Everything Is Sensual, *David Jauss* 128

Poem for People Who Are Understandably Too Busy to Read
    Poetry, *Stephen Dunn* 129
The Poem You Asked For, *Larry Levis* 131
The Poem in the Park, *Peter Davison* 132
To Build a Poem, *Christine E. Hemp* 133
Nude Reclining at Word Processor, in Pastel, *Carl
    Conover* 134
Back from the Word Processing Course, I Say to My Old
    Typewriter, *Michael Blumenthal* 135
Dancer, *Roy Scheele* 136
This poem is for Nadine, *Paul B. Janeczko* 137
On Addy Road, *May Swenson* 138
Walking with Your Eyes Shut, *William Stafford* 139
Markers, *Frank Steele* 139
Rollo's Miracle, *Paul Zimmer* 140
A Field Poem, *Laura Valaitis* 141

The One to Grieve, *Rudy Thomas* 142
A Dog in San Francisco, *Michael Ondaatje* 142
The Cats, *Samuel Exler* 143

Driving through Coal Country in Pennsylvania, *Jonathan
    Holden* 144
For Richard Chase, *Jim Wayne Miller* 144

Conquerors, *Henry Treece*   146
The Soldiers Returning, *Richard Shelton*   146
The Amputee Soldier, *Philip Dacey*   147

Winter Twilight, *Lou Lipsitz*   149
Full Moon, Rising, *Jonathan Holden*   149

At Midnight, *Ted Kooser*   151

Acknowledgments   152
Index to Poets   158

Going Over to Your Place

The Heart's Location

all my plans for suicide are ridiculous
I can never remember the heart's location
too cheap to smash the car
too queasy to slash a wrist
once jumped off a bridge
almost scared myself to death
then spent two foggy weeks
waiting for new glasses

of course I really want to live
continuing my lifelong search
for the world's greatest unknown cheap restaurant
and a poem full of ordinary words
about simple things
in the inconsolable rhythms of the heart

Part One

Storm Warnings

The glass has been falling all the afternoon,
And knowing better than the instrument
What winds are walking overhead, what zone
Of gray unrest is moving across the land,
I leave the book upon a pillowed chair
And walk from window to closed window, watching
Boughs strain against the sky

And think again, as often when the air
Moves inward toward a silent core of waiting,
How with a single purpose time has traveled
By secret currents of the undiscerned
Into this polar realm. Weather abroad
and weather in the heart alike come on
Regardless of prediction.

Between foreseeing and averting change
Lies all the mastery of elements
Which clocks and weatherglasses cannot alter.
Time in the hand is not control of time,
Nor shattered fragments of an instrument
A proof against the wind; the wind will rise,
We can only close the shutters.

I draw the curtains as the sky goes black
And set a match to candles sheathed in glass
Against the keyhole draught, the insistent whine
Of weather through the unsealed aperture.
This is our sole defense against the season;
These are the things that we have learned to do
Who live in troubled regions.

Spring Storm

He comes gusting out of the house,
the screen door a thunderclap behind him.

He moves like a black cloud
over the lawn and—stops.

A hand in his mind grabs
a purple crayon of anger
and messes the clean sky.

He sits on the steps, his eye drawing
a mustache on the face in the tree.

As his weather clears,
his rage dripping away,

wisecracks and wonderment
spring up like dandelions.

NANCY PRICE

One-Night Fair

A traveling fair pitched by our pasture gate
once. I still remember the Ferris wheel's
yellow lights going around the dark
like a slow mill, only it spilled a freight
of music-run, not water, and girls' squeals
from bucket seats. We rode that contraption late
and long as our nickels lasted. Like a lark
you rode that thing up to the music, hung

6

over our barn lot, pig pens; then you froze,
cleaving your way back down, a dead weight,
to fields you'd spent the years of your life among
and never seen before. It was one of those
one-night fairs, gone as quick as it came,
like love, maybe, or joy. Nobody knows
where it hailed from. It pitched here when I was young
and, like I say, I found out the way it feels
high up there, saw how the home place goes
turning under the night. There's no right name
for how it was. The farm's never looked the same.

❧

SHERYL L. NELMS

Into Fish

that teenage boy
who loiters
in the dark aisle
of every pet shop in town

gawky and awkward on land

becomes swift
and smooth

as he
breaks
the mirrored
surface of water

going down
through silver
bubbles

past the neons and gouramis

he glides
sleek in the spirit
of fish

while dissecting frogs in biology class
scrut discovers the intricacies of the
scooped neckline in his lab partner's dress

oh madame curie
oh louis pasteur

oh ponce de leon
and christopher columbus

you have nothing on me today

❧

SAMUEL HAZO

Between You and Me

A girl in yellow slacks kept watching me
as I slapped down a dime and palmed the three
lopsided baseballs just before I threw
and three times missed the pyramided pints.
I changed a dollar into dimes and threw
and missed again, but still the girl looked on
like someone waiting to applaud or boo.
Try throwing with a strange girl watching you.

Black-breasted Balinese, a bowl of gourds,
enormous trays for ashes, checker boards
and dolls attired as duchesses or nuns
sparkled like booty on the winner's shelf.
I threw and threw until my shirtback clung
adhesively and cold against my spine.
It was no more a case of having fun.
I swore I would keep throwing till I won.

9

I tried with all my will to concentrate
and pitched the final baseball hard and straight
at three damn target pints still left in line.
They broke like bottles shattered by a shot.
I turned to see if Yellow Slacks had seen,
but she was gone, and with her went my need
to win a wreath or some cheap figurine
to show the world, if you know what I mean.

NIKKI GIOVANNI

Kidnap Poem

ever been kidnapped
by a poet
if i were a poet
i'd kidnap you
put you in my phrases and meter
you to jones beach
or maybe coney island
or maybe just to my house
lyric you in lilacs
dash you into the beach
to complement my see
play the lyre for you
ode you with my love song
anything to win you
wrap you in the red Black green
show you off to mama
yeah if i were a poet i'd kid
nap you

First Kiss

The first girl I ever kissed was Sally Adams
on our third date. I was 13. I'd taken her
to *Battle Cry* with Aldo Ray.
Scarcely had the Looney Tunes cartoon come on
than we were in the usual position—
clutching hands, elbows, forearms all at once.
My left arm around her seat had gone to sleep,
when, silhouetted in the row in front,
this couple started wrestling in slow-motion.
You know how vampires, when they batten, fasten down?
That's what it looked like—on and on, his drooped head
lolling, rolling over hers until I thought, Ich!
Kissing that long's worse than holding hands; it's
messier! But I knew Sally saw them too. I
had to try. My heart began sprinting so hard
I was scared she heard it in my hot, tense hands.
To get across the space between two faces for the first
time's like standing on the high-dive, staring down.
You wish you'd jumped. You wonder if you'll dare.
My mouth was so dry I had to wet my lips. I sucked in
my breath, held it deep, launched out and down—
too late now to turn around—toward Sally's face, this
shy, dim crescent moon turning up toward me, becoming
full, with solemn eyes all filled with small, deep lights.
I heard distant gunshots, but I didn't care. I was
sinking. Her lashes grazed my cheek, and I realized
I was there. I'd landed not in a crash of water but
quietly, trembling, on the ground of this soft,
strange planet that seemed to move, to open under me.

First Love

At his incipient sun
The ice of twenty winters broke,
Crackling, in her eyes.

Her mirroring, still mind,
That held the world (made double) calm,
Went fluid, and it ran.

There was a stir of music,
Mixed with flowers, in her blood;
A swift impulsive balm

From obscure roots;
Gold bees of clinging light
Swarmed in her brow.

Her throat is full of songs,
She hums, she is sensible of wings
Growing on her heart.

She is a tree in spring
Trembling with the hope of leaves,
Of which the leaves are tongues.

❧

The Sound of Rain

Of all the secret places
to take a woman,
give me the condemned

ice house just off the
kill-floor of Armour's,
eight floors high,
and give me the sound of rain
on its tin roof.
It's dark inside,
nobody is around, and
there's a wooden bench.

And then give me Lurleen.
She is the hotter secret.
I'm half crazy about her
shiny rubber apron,
red bandana,
and how her wide sheath
of knives on her sagging belt
glitters like the Missouri.

I always imagine the rain's
skeleton fingers tapping
on that tin roof,
and us holding on to each other
in the condemned dark of Armour's.

Lurleen can't fool me.
The apron, bandana and knives
never did hide beauty from me.

At the St. Louis Institute
of Music

When Mr. Croxford
flicked his skinny wrist,
and the metronome began
its slow tick in his throat,
I knew that I was lost.
My thick hands tripped and stumbled
over the deviant keys,
my sour stomach off-key,
out of tune.
Outside, the day grew taut,
the fall air thin as wire,
and his voice, that cracked
and raspy sounding board,
sent me home.

All week I'd hear him clicking
out in center field, as
bases loaded, I'd pop up.
Or in the lunchroom,
flirting with the girls,
I'd feel his thin wrist
measuring my tongue until
his cracked voice rasped me back
and there I'd be again, legs
dangling from the stool,
wishing I had practiced.

Until one day they caught him
in the washroom
in a stall with Porky Brown,
and my short unhappy practice sessions ended.

I can't say I wasn't glad, or that
I felt much pity for him:
I made first string and several girls
and easily forgot him.
Yet, years later, safely married,
on days flat and diminished,
as I practice my profession
in the silence of my room,
I miss the crazy bastard,
and wish him back to abuse me
into song.

&

JEFF WORLEY

Whitley at Three O'Clock

He hadn't been right
all that winter. Victim
of the ABC's, he sat
at the far corner of vision,
last seat, last row: Whitley.
Same buckskin shirt
dancing with lassos, hands
like duststorms, always
a mouthful of Black Jack away
from any answer.

Miss Lytton set the portable
blackboard spinning
with a universe of closed
brackets, absolutes, congruents,
logic of greater, logic of less,
unknown x's and y's and z's
disappearing, reassembling

15

on the other side
their found identities.

She placed the chalk in its
grooved cradle, the dust
of creativity settling around her.
Wiped her black-rimmed glasses.

(Whitley made his move:
to pencil sharpener and—
sleight of hand, chalk,
eraser—back.)

Her face scanned the room
for an arm breaking
the surface of air, for any
factors of uncertainty.

"You never know
when you might be tested."

The sabotaged eraser nestled
into her palm. And we waited
the arrival of Whitley's Comet,
the sudden spine-screeching
tingle of meaning, the white
lie already forming
like a blister on his lips.

Empty Holds a Question

I saw him brought into Emergency,
reduced, behind his life-pressed scowl, to fear.
He'd been my teacher of geometry—
a tall, proud man behind a quizzing frown,
who'd pulled the theorems off the printed page
and called Infinity to being in my mind.
He'd said, "All things can be, quite logically,
defined with mathematics."
I was the one white uniform that wore a face—
he trusted me and signed the space that he'd refused before.
Presurgery, I took his pulse, all platitudes and hope . .
But he did not return . . .
And so,
could not trace out for me
how I could be at twenty-two
as old as all mankind.

Poet in Residence at a
Country School

The school greets me like a series
of sentence fragments sent out to recess.
Before I hit the front door
I'm into a game of baseball soccer.
My first kick's a foul; my second sails
over the heads of the outfielders;
rounding third base, I suck in my stomach
and dodge the throw of a small blue-eyed boy.
I enter the school, sucking apples of wind.
In the fifth-grade section of the room
I stand in the center of an old rug and ask,
Where would you go where no one could find you,
a secret place where you'd be invisible
to everyone except yourselves?
What would you do there; what would you say?
I ask them to imagine they're there,
and writing a poem. As I walk around the room,
I look at the wrists of the kids,
green and alive, careful with silence.
They are writing themselves into fallen elms,
corners of barns, washouts, and alkali flats.
I watch until a tiny boy approaches,
who says he can't think of a place,
who wonders today, at least,
if he just couldn't sit on my lap.
Tomorrow, he says, he'll write.

And so the two of us sit under a clock,
beside a gaudy picture of a butterfly,
and a sweet poem of Christina Rosetti's.
And in all that silence, neither of us
can imagine where he'd rather be.

৵

JAMES B. HATHAWAY

What the Stone Dreams

for Naomi

Pacing back & forth between their restless
little bodies, I ask my students
to imagine that they are stones, to tell
me what the stones dream. I pace
a little more & one says "I don't know
what stones dream" & another says "Everyone
knows that stones *don't* dream." The sun
blasts at the playground & the yard's glare
blasts the room. "Just imagine," I tell them,
"that you are a stone, lying belly down, stuck
to your ears in nice, cool clay. You are near
the top off a round grassy hill, the sky is blue,
the breeze is blowing the clouds over you."
I look at them again & see that most
are already dreaming; one thinks that it would
be nice to be a stone, to be hard, to break other
stones; one imagines lying deep, deep underground,
where it is so dark & quiet that one can sleep
& sleep, never having to move; one dreams that he
is a stone, dreaming that he is a toad, hunkered
down to the soft ground, hiding from a fox. Me, I can't
help it, but I start dreaming too, dreaming that
I am a child again, back in the cool of fall.

I think of blue October Saturdays, carrying
a big brown paper bag to Library Slope, to the old
chestnut trees, where I would sit, popping open
the thorny cases, tearing at the brown spines,
showing the soft milky flesh beneath, & beneath
that the hard shiny lump of the chestnut, the seed
miraculously cool like a perfect stone in the palm
of my hand. While the sun tried to beat through the heavy
green of the chestnut leaves, while the faint roar
of the crowd in the stadium melted down the hill,
I filled my bag. When I was done, it was heavier than
I could handle. Still, I carried the bag home, trudging
under the load, until the paper finally tore.
I sat there in the grass, in the pile of my polished
booty, happy, feeling their mysterious coolness,
imagining that I was one of those peaceful stones.

ALDEN NOWLAN

He Sits Down on the Floor of a School for the Retarded

I sit down on the floor of a school for the retarded,
a writer of magazine articles accompanying a band
that was met at the door by a child in a man's body
who asked them, "Are you the surprise they promised us?"

It's Ryan's Fancy, Dermot on guitar,
Fergus on banjo, Denis on penny-whistle.
In the eyes of this audience, they're everybody
who has ever appeared on TV. I've been telling lies
to a boy who cried because his favorite detective
hadn't come with us; I said he had sent his love
and, no, I didn't think he'd mind if I signed his name

to a scrap of paper: when the boy took it, he said,
"Nobody will ever get this away from me,"
in the voice, more hopeless than defiant,
of one accustomed to finding that his hiding places
have been discovered, used to having objects snatched
out of his hands. Weeks from now I'll send him
another autograph, this one genuine
in the sense of having been signed by somebody
on the same payroll as the star.
Then I'll feel less ashamed. Now everyone is singing,
"Old MacDonald had a farm," and I don't know what to do
about the young woman (I call her a woman
because she's twenty-five at least, but think of her
as a little girl, she plays that part so well,
having known no other), about the young woman who
sits down beside me and, as if it were the most natural
thing in the world, rests her head on my shoulder.

It's nine o'clock in the morning, not an hour for music.
And, at the best of times, I'm uncomfortable
in situations where I'm ignorant
of the accepted etiquette: it's one thing
to jump a fence, quite another thing to blunder
into one in the dark. I look around me
for a teacher to whom to smile out my distress.
They're all busy elsewhere, "Hold me," she whispers. "Hold me."

I put my arm around her. "Hold me tighter."
I do, and she snuggles closer, I half-expect
someone in authority to grab her
or me; I can imagine this being remembered
for ever as the time the sex-crazed writer
publicly fondled the poor retarded girl.
"Hold me," she says again. What does it matter
what anybody thinks? I put my other arm around her,
rest my chin in her hair, thinking of children,

real children, and of how they say it, "Hold me,"
and of a patient in a geriatric ward
I once heard crying out to his mother, dead
for half a century, "I'm frightened! Hold me!"
and of a boy-soldier screaming it on the beach
at Dieppe, of Nelson in Hardy's arms,
of Frieda gripping Lawrence's ankle
until he sailed off in his Ship of Death.

It's what we all want, in the end,
to be held, merely to be held,
to be kissed (not necessarily with the lips,
for every touching is a kind of kiss).

Yet, it's what we all want, in the end,
not to be worshipped, not to be admired,
not to be famous, not to be feared,
not even to be loved, but simply to be held.

She hugs me now, this retarded woman, and I hug her.
We are brother and sister, father and daughter,
mother and son, husband and wife.
We are lovers. We are two human beings
huddled together for a little while by the fire
in the Ice Age, two hundred thousand years ago.

SAMUEL HAZO

To a Blind Student Who Taught Me to See

More reminiscent than distressed, you say
you recollect the pain of sight as I
might dream of buried men whose living hands

I shook, faces I knew, voices I heard
and hear again when I remember them.
You feel no urge to resurrect one day

when you could see a stucco chimney webbed
with rosevines, trios of basted, browning hens
revolving slowly backward on a spit,
the way a collie's torso thrust ahead
and instantly recoiled from its bark.
You claim the world is nearer in the dark.

This makes me think that Oedipus was blind
before he gouged his eyeballs from his skull.
No longer blinded by the visible,
he turned two hollow sockets on a dusk
of light he had to blind himself to see.
I draw from this that only in the mind

is there a world, and never two the same,
that blind men walk with cautious dignity
partly from need, partly because they know
the single world is multiple as men's
imaginings, that streets are nothing but
the way we picture them, that doors can shut

or open if we twist the keys or not.
Your blindness makes me memorize with you
the accidental braille of time and place
until I see how Homer saw a world
of iliads and odysseys arise
like magic to the tapping cane of thought.

Myrtle

Wearing her yellow rubber slicker,
Myrtle, our *Journal* carrier,
has come early through rain and darkness
to bring us the news.
A woman of thirty or so,
with three small children at home,
she's told me she likes
a long walk by herself in the morning.
And with pride in her work,
she's wrapped the news neatly in plastic—
a bread bag, beaded with rain,
that reads WONDER.
From my doorway I watch her
flicker from porch to porch as she goes,
a yellow candle flame
no wind or weather dare extinguish.

❧

For Wilma

Quasimodo loomed
behind the racks of *Upper Rooms*
and hymnals at our church's door
when I watched Wilma Gibbeaut
ring the bell. More hunched
than hunchbacked, she assumed
over the years the shape
of the bell itself:
the chopped grey hair,

the tucked head blending
with the cowbird-colored coat
she wore year round.
She had a face Lon Chaney
would have envied—
turtle eyes
and teeth
like wind-eroded locust posts.

She lived alone
though stories coupled her
with Sweat Carruthers in his barn:
creature love thumping dust
off the tow sacks—grainy one reelers
with the only man in town
who still drove mules.

She never missed a Sunday
and some days when I arrived
before the final call,
she'd wink
and hand the rope to me
and let the bell's backswing
lift me
through the stalled choir,
through rafters,
roof, belfry
and beyond.

On Being Much Better Than Most and Yet Not Quite Good Enough

There was a great swimmer named Jack
Who swam ten miles out—and nine back.

The Man Who Owned Cars

It began
reasonably enough.
His wife did need her own car.
Then he bought a third
as a backup.
As he drove the streets alone at night
he saw them everywhere,
moon glinting off rounded hoods,
FOR SALE signs clamped by ragged wipers,
pale plump sedans
abandoned like double-chinned lovers.

He felt sorry for them,
bought a couple,
changed their murky oil,
prowled time-capsuled trunks.
   "They're cheap," he told his wife.
   "Cheaper than hamburger."
      "But what will you do with them?"
   "Fix them up and sell them."

But he never did.
Always something kept them from the block,
slumbering batteries or dazed valves.
He felt sorry for weepy radiators and fat bald tires,
and bought more,
'62 Imperials with Buck Rogers Raygun taillights,
aging Lincolns whose slab sides resembled the decks
of sinking Japanese carriers,
angular Cadillacs whose chrome-sopped fins threatened
annihilation to quivering Toyotas.
He sat in them, sniffed the sweet scent of leaking gas,
fondled cracked leather, listened to the metronome
of chromed eccentric clocks.
    "They're relics of another time. Look
    at those hubcaps—sculpture."
        "The neighbors are complaining," she replied.

He bought flaking Buicks with sagging doors
whose radio tubes last winked
to Edward R. Murrow saying Yes, the Russians
have the bomb,
whose heaters were Iron Curtain cold.
        "But you don't even drive them," she said.
    "That's not the point. Must you drive
    something or eat it or live in it
    before it has value?"
        "But what about the neighbors?"

He shrugged—she didn't
understand. He began taking
late night drivers past blackened gas stations,
watched tankers furtively coast and pant
out their loads before chuffing lightly
into dark.

He drove until the morning papers were delivered
to liquor stores in huge soft stacks,
then pulled one from wire bindings,
checked the ads. A Buick for breakfast,
a Lincoln for lunch.

His wife did not speak any more,
only shuffled silently through rooms filled with radiators,
fenders, and the exhaust system of a '58 Plymouth Fury.
     Finally she said, "It's me or them."
   "Let me think about it," he replied,
and took a drive. A Plymouth Barracuda later,
he read a black sign, WAREHOUSE FOR RENT.
Fate, he thought. Moved them all in, bought
a '57 El Dorado to celebrate. He felt sorry for it.
The angular fins seemed so pathetic, like
a sparrow's broken wings.

He used the trunks as closets, kept socks
in the Imperials, underwear in the Lincolns,
shirts and pants in the Cads.
With a hot plate he got by, slept in back seats.
Sundays he rode each one through the car wash,
liked the warm sudsy spray and the brushes all over him at once.

Days slid by bright and smooth as polished chrome.
Nights in his corrugated harem he had so many lovers
it was nearly impossible to choose.

♀

Laughing Backwards

Laughter helped me keep my spirits up during a
very difficult period

NORMAN COUSINS

The first thing I ever knew was funny
was Sylvester Keach who walked backwards.
Sixty or so, pudgy, bald, six feet tall, who
walked backwards along the shoulder smiling at
the cars, walked backwards from his mother's place
way out on Cox Mill Road down to Ninth and Main,
then turned around and walked backwards home.

Sometimes we'd drive up to Sylvester
in Paul's Packard and honk or throw a cherry
bomb nearby, and he'd laugh and wave and keep on
walking, picking his way backwards
to town or backwards back to home.

Laugh? We laughed until we couldn't spit or speak,
and once, Paul drove us along beside
old Sylvester, driving in reverse and us all sitting
backwards in our seats. And Sylvester Keach
laughed so hard, laughed and laughed
he nearly lurched into a shrub.

You expect things like this to turn out sad,
and to look back and say, Gawd
we were little monsters to treat poor Sylvester
so pitifully, and thank the Lord we know better now.

But the joke is, Sylvester Keach walked backwards
right up till he died at 86, and his last afternoon
he'd walked backwards into town and waved at every

honking teenager and smelled the sweet gun powder
grit of cherry bombs, and laughed his hearty laugh
that anybody'd be happy to laugh on their last day.

And you'd like to think all the funeral cars drove
backwards, and they lowered him upside down
into his hole and stood around laughing,
and then drove backwards home, slinging cherry bombs
at all those tragic fools picking their way forward.

Part Two

Living with Children

Sorcerers, they've turned
the house into a serialized fairy tale.
The plot, full of reversals,
mysterious messages, unfolds
day after day, surprising
as fried marbles underfoot.

A frog on the floor, waiting to be kissed.
A rabbit, a pet snake.
Half a sandwich shelved with books.
Ghosts, guns, flowers.
Winged, web-footed snakes drawn
on the walls of bedrooms, their caves.

There is an enchanted forest inhabited
by Crayola people who fear
the heat of the sun and never venture
from under their Crayola trees—so different

from the watercolor folk, who live
in an eternal spring, standing forever
in watercolor puddles, hands reaching up
to a sun that looks down on them,
a blissful idiot.

In my desk drawer, an unfamiliar
piece of paper that accordions out:
"Don't touch this or you'll die!"

It's too late.

First Song

Then it was dusk in Illinois, the small boy
After an afternoon of carting dung
Hung on the rail fence, a sapped thing
Weary to crying. Dark was growing tall
And he began to hear the pond frogs all
Calling on his ear with what seemed their joy.

Soon their sound was pleasant for a boy
Listening in the smoky dusk and the nightfall
Of Illinois, and from the fields two small
Boys came bearing cornstalk violins
And they rubbed the cornstalk bows with resins
And the three sat there scraping of their joy.

It was not fine music the frogs and the boys
Did in the towering Illinois twilight make
And into dark in spite of a shoulder's ache
A boy's hunched body loved out of a stalk
The first song of his happiness, and the song woke
His heart to the darkness and into the sadness of joy.

JOHN M. RODERICK

Passage

He was older and
I stood behind him in frozen pride,
Straining my eyes into the towering branches,
Unable to see what he saw.

34

His hand coiled around the air rifle
In a serpentine embrace
That welded his face against the gunstock.

"What is it?" broke the silence
But not his concentration
Or his slow, steady aim.

The shot was more like a puff than a bang,
A soft sudden breath of air
That sent its lethal message through the leaves.

"You missed!" I said,
Though I didn't know what.
"I never miss, kid."

And then to prove he was right
A small sparrow fell to the ground
With blood at its throat.

My own blood surged
To be so close to death . . .
But the sparrow lived!

"It's not dead!" caught in my throat
As the bird's heart
Pumped out a bib of crimson.

"Not yet," he said
And squeezed a thumb into its throat until
I could not breathe.

The Biplane

for Rolly Kent

Sometimes the night is not enough. I rise remembering,
And the dream is no longer a quaint story
In another's life, but my own grown more real.
Last night a biplane landed in my neighbor's field.
I watched, from my window seat, the canvas wings
Graze the rows of corn and come to rest.
                                        Afternoons
Seem always time between the crests of dream. There is
An oak outside my window so stunted, its limbs
Elbowing this way and that, it seems it had made
A decision not to grow beyond its needs. In spring
The leaves appear, in fall they yellow and curl,
And I know the constant change in direction is a
Ruse to make it seem more humble.
                                    Again last night
The biplane landed in my neighbor's field.
It caught fire, but when the wind finally blew
It out, I felt like the child who snuffs a match
In a closet and finds himself alone and bodiless.
Just think: I forgot the dream today. I woke
And drank my coffee, washed, put on my clothes;
On the way to work, I stopped and turned back,

But couldn't think what it was I had forgotten.
It was like the biplane from World War I.
Beyond the window, the tree was waving its arms.
A pilot from long ago, wearing my father's cap
And goggles, was waving his arms. Now I remember.

It was my father's dream, told to me as a child,
Put on like a coat that one day fits. I rise from
My window seat. Remember the child who wanted never
To grow up? The child has gone and found his way.

To My Daughter Riding in the Circus Parade

("Reporter Catherine Schutz . . . an editor's
assignment put her atop an elephant . . ." *The
Contra Costa Independent*, Richmond, California)

Once, more than you wanted
the moon or the stars,
you wanted a rabbit.
Your father brought one home,
a scared snowball of fluff,
to nest in your eager arms.
You were ecstatic.
You were determined to ride a mule
down into the Grand Canyon,
and you did,
while I, already pinched
in the dull vise of caution,
waited nervously at the rim.
You wanted to dance
in a musical comedy,
and there you were,
looking owlish without your glasses
and flashing your high kicks
with a Rockette's verve.
And now, my dear,
that you're thirty, and settled,
and should know better,
you've erupted again—a star
in every girl's fantasy—
spangled in pink sequins, trying
to steady your headdress
while you keep a precarious balance
on the back of an elephant.

And I, who have loved you through
each translation
of child to girl to woman,
can only applaud, saluting
your untamed heart,
that does not know it knows
there's an end to dreaming.

MICHAEL ONDAATJE

To a Sad Daughter

All night long the hockey pictures
gaze down at you
sleeping in your tracksuit.
Belligerent goalies are your ideal.
Threats of being traded
cuts and wounds
—all this pleases you.
O *my god!* you say at breakfast
reading the sports page over the Alpen
as another player breaks his ankle
or assaults the coach.

When I thought of daughters
I wasn't expecting this
but I like this more.
I like all your faults
even your purple moods
when you retreat from everyone
to sit in bed under a quilt.
And when I say "like"
I mean of course "love"
but that embarrasses you.

You who feel superior to black and white movies
(coaxed for hours to see *Casablanca*)
though you were moved
by *Creature from the Black Lagoon.*

One day I'll come swimming
beside your ship or someone will
and if you hear the siren
listen to it. For if you close your ears
only nothing happens. You will never change.

I don't care if you risk
your life to angry goalies
creatures with webbed feet.
You can enter their caves and castles
their glass laboratories. Just
don't be fooled by anyone but yourself.

This is the first lecture I've given you.
You're "sweet sixteen" you said.
I'd rather be your closest friend
than your father. I'm not good at advice
you know that, but ride
the ceremonies
until they grow dark.

Sometimes you are so busy
discovering your friends
I ache with a loss
—but that is greed.
And sometimes I've gone
into *my* purple world
and lost you.

One afternoon I stepped
into your room. You were sitting
at the desk where I now write this.

Forsythia outside the window
and sun spilled over you
like a thick yellow miracle
as if another planet
was coaxing you out of the house
—all those possible worlds!—
and you, meanwhile, busy with mathematics.

I cannot look at forsythia now
without loss, or joy for you.
You step delicately
into the wild world
and your real prize will be
the frantic search.
Want everything. If you break
break going out not in.
How you live your life I don't care
but I'll sell my arms for you,
hold your secrets forever.

If I speak of death
which you fear now, greatly,
it is without answers,
except that each
one we know is
in our blood.
Don't recall graves.
Memory is permanent.
Remember the afternoon's
yellow suburban annunciation.
Your goalie
in his frightening mask
dreams perhaps
of gentleness.

Departing Words to a Son

We choose to say goodbye against our will
Home will take on stillness when you're gone
Remember us—but don't dwell on the past
Here—wear this watch my father gave to me

Home will take on stillness when you're gone
We'll leave your room as is—at least for now
Here—wear this watch my father gave to me
His face dissolves within the whirling snow

We'll leave your room as is—at least for now
I'll dust the model boats that sail your wall
His face dissolves within the whirling snow
It's hard to picture someone else's life

I'll dust the model boats that sail your wall
Don't lose the watch—the inside is engraved
It's hard to picture someone else's life
Your window's full of icicles again

Don't lose the watch—the inside is engraved
A wedge of geese heads somewhere out of sight
Your window's full of icicles again
Look how the icicles reflect the moon

A wedge of geese heads somewhere out of sight
My father knew the distances we keep
Look how the icicles reflect the moon
The moonlight shimmers wave-like on your wall

My father knew the distances we keep
Your mother sometimes cries out in the night
The moonlight shimmers wave-like on your wall
One June I dove too deep and nearly drowned

42

Your mother sometimes cries out in the night
She dreams the windy snow has covered her
One June I dove too deep and nearly drowned
She says she's watched me shudder in my sleep

She dreams the windy snow has covered her
She's heard your lost scream stretch across the snow
She says she's watched me shudder in my sleep
We all conceive the loss of what we love

She's heard your lost scream stretch across the snow
My need for her clenched tighter at your birth
We all conceive the loss of what we love
Our love for you has given this house breath

My need for her clenched tighter at your birth
Stillness deepens pulsing in our veins
Our love for you has given this house breath
Some day you'll pass this watch on to your son

Stillness deepens pulsing in our veins
My father's words still speak out from the watch
Some day you'll pass this watch on to your son
Repeating what the goldsmith has etched there

My father's words still speak out from the watch
As moonlit icicles drip on your sill
Repeating what the goldsmith has etched there
We choose to say goodbye against our will

❧

Father to Son

I do not understand this child
Though we have lived together now
In the same house for years. I know
Nothing of him, so try to build
Up a relationship from how
He was when small. Yet have I killed

The seed I spent or sown it where
The land is his and none of mine?
We speak like strangers, there's no sign
Of understanding in the air.
This child is built to my design
Yet what he loves I cannot share.

Silence surrounds us. I would have
Him prodigal, returning to
His father's house, the home he knew,
Rather than see him make and move
His world. I would forgive him too,
Shaping from sorrow a new love.

Father and son, we both must live
On the same globe and the same land.
He speaks: I cannot understand
Myself, why anger grows from grief.
We each put out an empty hand,
Longing for something to forgive.

A Child's Grave Marker

A small block of granite
engraved with her name and the dates
just wasn't quite pretty enough
for this lost little girl
or her parents, who added a lamb
cast in plaster of paris,
using the same kind of cake mold
my grandmother had—iron,
heavy and black as a skillet.
The lamb came out coconut-white,
and seventy years have proven it
soft in the rain. On this hill,
overlooking a river in Iowa,
it melts in its own sweet time.

Lament

my old red schwinn had a carrier over the back fender
on your first day gail i would ride you to school
you would hold my side with one hand and balance
our lunch sacks in the other your legs dangling
outside the flashing spokes we would talk and laugh
if it should suddenly rain i would give you my jacket

but by three years old your heart had grown too large
for your body i never rode you on my bike i
never took you to school i am afraid to go there
myself now and my heart is the reverse of yours
sister it is growing smaller

GEORGE BOGIN

Abraham

Abraham was the name
of my stillborn brother.
Pink and beautiful,
my mother would say sadly
who saw him only for a moment
before he was removed.
My grandfather brought him
to a small grave
and named him there.
I don't know
if there was a tombstone.

Everyone is dead who would know
the little there is to know
about Abraham.

BARON WORMSER

For My Brother Who Died
Before I Was Born

Pearly and opaque boy, it was to you
To whom as a god
I furtively prayed before
I launched an aggie
Or played a decisive card.

I made lists of the reasons why:
Certain teachers and times of the year
And the failure of my team
To score runners from third—
Those were all things to make you die.

I meant to discover
My own mortality.
I mocked my mocking breath
And deftly smoked
Too many cigarettes.
At night I heard footsteps, high-pitched
Voices. Once I saw a face in a candle flame.

Your absence was a game
Which might at any move
Intrude upon my wanting life.
My hand fit in your old ball glove.
My dream was real:
Imagination is the proof of love.

A Man of Action

In 1933 my parents won in a raffle
a new Terraplane. That's a car, now extinct,
as are my parents, essentially.
In the backseat were two bushelbaskets,
one filled with fruit, the other with canned goods.
My father put the food out, the kids in,
then motored us on a Sunday drive,
a term also now in Dodo bird country.

Rolling along at a spiffy 35 mph through
the museum-case Pennsylvania countryside
the family was a Norman Rockwell magazine cover—until:
my paper whistle refused to blow.
Instead of puffing out, I sucked in.
The metal part dislodged. I gagged and choked.
"Stop the car, Charlie! He's turning blue."
(Strange, that is still my favorite color.)
Calmly, as he did all things, my father
pulled off the road, came in back,
and with his forefinger forced me to swallow.
It was the only thing he ever shoved down my throat.

JACK DRISCOLL

Arm Wrestling with My Father

We lean across the kitchen table,
so late
        the moon outside grips the clear ice
hardening on the pond.
My father's strength is in his eyes.

49

He stares at me
and I know I can never win by pinning his thin arm,
that he squeezes my schoolteacher hand as if to explain
how little my visit each winter
relieves his sadness working all year
alone on this farm.

He whispers, "GO,"
and the full weight of our bodies heaves
in opposite directions,
the thermometer at the window holding
exactly at zero.
            Now his wrist bends and
as if suddenly dancing, our foreheads touch.
For that moment we let go of the distance between us
like two men who have just shaken hands
in a small room
and have turned slowly away to watch the stars
without counting losses.

GEORGE ELLA LYON

A Testimony

for L. H.

My Daddy baptized me
in the Redbird River.
We waded into green water
—him in his preaching pants,
shirt sleeves rolled up high,
me in a white dress
that hung like a pillowslip.

You know my daddy
was no more holy

than that car up on blocks.
The middle of the night might find him
sneaking out of town
or a trespassed bed.
But all the same his baptizing
did me good.
                    I liked the ache
of his voice when he prayed in the river,
how everyone sang, mournful and drenched
from the ooze of cattails and willows.
And his handkerchief over my nose
smelling of the iron in Mama's hand,
his palm cradling my neck
as he bent me back and under

Through the arc
of green-fringed blue,
a world I knew I was leaving,
into the all of water, cold,
his hands bore me
down.

⚘

DAVID HUDDLE

Stopping by Home

1.

Five times since July my father
has been hospitalized. He's home
today, sitting up at his desk
in bathrobe, pajamas, slippers.
I am embarrassed, I want him
fat again, in khakis that smell
like sweat, cigarette smoke, carbide,

ignoring me because he'd rather
work the crossword puzzle, alone
or pretending to be, than risk
in those minutes before supper
finding out what meanness I'd been
up to. He's thin now. And pale.
Waiting to hear what's on my mind.

2.

In the summer in the hospital
he sat on the bed's edge clutching
that Formica table they crank up
and put your food tray on. He coughed
up white mucus, took oxygen
from a thin green tube, couldn't sleep,
couldn't lie back and breathe. He

and my mother thought it was all
finished the day he got medicine
to make him relax, make him sleep,
then couldn't sit up because he'd lost
his strength but couldn't breathe lying
back. They rang for the nurse, but he
passed through something you couldn't see.

3.

They say his hair turned white. It's true,
it's grayer than it was, almost
white. He can't read much now, has no
power of concentration, mind
strays. Today he talks about friends
who've died, relatives long gone.
In a photograph he points out

which ones are dead now. "But you
and Lester Waller and Tom Pope
and George Schreiber and James Payne—so
many still alive," I remind
him. He seems not to hear and bends
to put the picture away. "Some
still around," he says, "yes, no doubt."

4.
My mother wants us to talk. This
is what she always wants, her sons
sitting around with their dad, talk
being evidence of love, she
thinks. My evenings home from school,
the army, New York, or Vermont,
she'd leave the room for us to do it.

We always argued politics.
Didn't intend to, but reasons
came to us. Once he said I ought
to go to Russia if the
things I said were really true,
and I walked out. Words are too hard
for us now. We'll just have to sit.

5.

Their lives in that house before he got too sick must have been
so filled with silence that even when a truck would pass
on the highway down the hill they would listen. Those
clear sunny days of May and June she sat with him
on the front porch where sometimes the soft wind
rustled in that hackberry that's grown
so high now. I hold an infant

recollection of the sun
warming the three of us,
their holding me so
close between them
I knew then
what home
meant.

6.

So
if I
care so much
about them I
have to sit up here
a thousand miles away
and write myself back home, why

not look for a job down there, try
to find some town close enough to say,
"I'm going to see them," drive over there
and walk in the door and not even surprise
them, sit down with them and talk, maybe stay for lunch,
say an easy goodbye and leave without feeling like
I betrayed them, and I will never find my way back home.

7.

Night comes down, the winter sky
momentarily ecstatic,
then stunned, bruised, ruined with pain, dark . . .
Coal on the fire, our old habits
keep us still, without lights, sitting
until the study's bay window
yields maybe one moving tree branch.

Then Mother rises, breathes a sigh
for all three of us when she flicks
on the overhead light. The dog barks
lightly in its sleep. We blink. It's
not late. His fingers shake setting
his watch. Before us are the slow
hours, each breath he takes a chance.

8.

At six we move from the study
to the living room for the news,
the weather report our excuse.
The man draws snow over the whole
Northeast, freely uses the word
blizzard, and I stand up before
he's finished and say I think I

better keep driving north, maybe
I can beat that storm. "But son, you
just got here." Mother's hurt. He's used
to my skedaddling ways, and so
makes himself grin, offers his hand
for me to shake and at the door
we say our word for love. Goodbye.

9.

I scuttle out into the dark
and drive three hundred miles north, numb,
knowing that I hurt but not able
to register it, a busted
speedometer on a car that
hurtles forward. In the morning
I get what's coming to me. Snow

starts in Pennsylvania, slick
stuff on those mountains south of Scranton,
the interstate a long white table
of ice, everything blasted
white. Wind and drifts in those high flat
stretches near nowhere. Endless dream
of losing control, moving through snow.

10.

Tell me whose parents don't get old.
Your father's sick, and you can't stand
to be around him and help him
die or get well, whichever it
turns out he's going to do. Well,
son, you deserve to drive through snow,
wind and freezing cold, past Hometown,

Port Jervis, Newburgh, Kingston. No
decent motel would have you, can't
stop, can't give your old man an arm
to help him walk into the next
room. Albany says go to hell,
keep driving, boy, get your ass home
where you've got children of your own.

Tunes for Bears to Dance To

For the third time in ten years
my father is dying. First
bladder infections, then pneumonia, and now
a single improbable bedsore, and once more
the doctors are shaking their stethoscopes
and muttering "no hope."
My mother says, as she's said before,
she'd rather he were gone
than lying helpless forever
with his catheter and pills
and the fixed routine his only
dependable visitors.
But I don't know.
Has his paralysis spread so far
he can't move even us?
Ten years ago I wept, and careless
of embarrassment or futility,
railed at the pale, indifferent sky.
Five years ago I grieved
more for myself, for my cool, detached
poetic eye.
Today, I am merely reasonable and calm
as the inevitable 2 A.M. telephone
tells me the terrible news:
a festering bedsore has burst
to the surface, shredding his skin
like lettuce; his tailbone is
a thin spike of rot.
The doctors are appalled.
It should never have happened,
should have been
avoidable. They are wrong.

It is never avoidable.
The human heart one day stops beating
out its tunes for bears to dance to,
as if it knows that only silence
could finally move the stars to pity.

NORMA HOPE RICHMAN

A Daughter's House

in memory of my mother

"That which thy fathers have bequeathed to thee,
earn it anew if thou wouldst possess it."

GOETHE: Faust
epigraph, Joy of Cooking, *1964*

Because of you, I'm an heiress
though I go to an office each day.
I have a 2½-pound Vita Herring jar of buttons,
more buttons than I shall ever have occasion to attach
to anything, and most of them older than I am.
I don't sew.
I open the jar and smell.
There you are: the Singer with the knee peddle
is playing its song. Loretta Young is on t.v.
A row or two of rickrack can lift things
out of the realm of the ordinary.

Because of you, I own many cookbooks
some with flour pressed inside for twenty years
and kitchen-tested annotations
in a script that mine resembles.
You'll find no pot roasts here
among the jars of grain and soaking lentils,

58

but sometimes I go to your books
to see the floury pages like parched old earth
from which nothing new can spring.
My crazy green kitchen gets a cloud of white dust.
Hello.

Manners

For a child of 1918

My grandfather said to me
as we sat on the wagon seat,
"Be sure to remember to always
speak to everyone you meet."

We met a stranger on foot.
My grandfather's whip tapped his hat.
"Good day, sir. Good day. A fine day."
And I said it and bowed where I sat.

Then we overtook a boy we knew
with his big pet crow on his shoulder.
"Always offer everyone a ride;
don't forget that when you get older,"

my grandfather said. So Willy
climbed up with us, but the crow
gave a "Caw!" and flew off. I was worried.
How would he know where to go?

But he flew a little way at a time
from fence post to fence post, ahead;
and when Willy whistled he answered.
"A fine bird," my grandfather said,

"and he's well brought up. See, he answers
nicely when he's spoken to.
Man or beast, that's good manners.
Be sure that you both always do."

When automobiles went by,
the dust hid the people's faces,
but we shouted "Good day! Good day!
Fine day!" at the top of our voices.

When we came to Hustler Hill,
he said that the mare was tired,
so we all got down and walked,
as our good manners required.

DAVID HUDDLE

Shooting Crows

Mostly it was starlings
and grackles that landed in
those trees of an evening,
but we called them crows,
and I'd sit out there on
the side of Broomsage Hill,
waiting for Grandad to take
a shot at them, which he
would do two or three times
before it got dark. Now
and then he'd hit one, I'd
watch it fall, tear off over
there under the tree to try
to get a look, once grandly
horrified to see it flapping
spattering red splotches on
the milkweed leaves, and I
couldn't understand why he
never wanted to see a dead
one, didn't even try all that

61

hard to hit one, would just
sit sit there in his khaki work
clothes and smoke one Camel
after another and spit now
and then, try to tease me
about that red-headed Delby
girl I wasn't even slightly
interested in. I like how
it smelled, though, after he
shot and he'd let me chamber
the fat shells for him. And
once he even let me have a
sip of what he was drinking
though he cautioned me twice
not to let the old battle ax,
by which he meant my grandmama,
find out about it.

GEORGE ELLA LYON

My Grandfather in Search
of Moonshine

For once he wanted
some high quality white
to keep on the pantry shelf
back behind beans and corn
to reach for and apply
whenever the wound came open.
So he asked his brother-in-law, Jim,
what door he should knock on.
Jim sent him up the creek.
He'd hardly got his feet set
for climbing that rooty staircase

when he met a stranger coming down,
beard thick and under his arm
a shoebox tied with twine.

"Evening, I'm looking for some moonshine.
You know of any up this way?"
"Don't know as I do." He pulled at his beard.
"But five dollars might find some."
The bill passed.
The man handed him the box.
"Wait here, and hold these shoes."

He waited. He walked, whistled, chewed,
spat grasshoppers off stones.
Quarter hour passed, then half,
earthclock winding its shadows:
no grisly man, no jar
with its creekwater turned to song.
He felt anger under his ribs,
fire at the edge of a field.
He cursed, kicked rocks,
wiped fool-sweat from his face.
"Least I've got his shoes," he thought.
"That's something, if they fit."
He cut the twine with his pocket knife,
lifted the dusty lid. There was his jar.
"I'll be damned," he said,
opened it and drank,
turning like a twig on a spider strand
hung plumb-bob for the web.

Grandmother Grace

I didn't give her a good-bye kiss
as I went off in the bus for the last time,
away from her house in Williamsburg, Iowa,
away from her empty house with Jesus
on all of the walls, with clawfoot tub and sink,
with the angular rooms that trapped all my summers.

I remember going there every summer—
every day beginning with that lavender kiss,
that face sprayed and powdered at the upstairs sink,
then mornings of fragile teacups and old times,
afternoons of spit-moistened hankies and Jesus,
keeping me clean in Williamsburg, Iowa.

Cast off, abandoned, in Williamsburg, Iowa,
I sat in that angular house with summer
dragging me onward, hearing how Jesus
loved Judas despite his last kiss,
how he turned his other cheek time after time,
how God wouldn't let the good person sink.

Months later, at Christmas, my heart would sink
when that flowery letter from Williamsburg, Iowa,
arrived, insistent, always on time,
stiff and perfumed as summer.
She always sealed it with a kiss,
a taped-over dime, and the words of Jesus.

I could have done without the words of Jesus;
the dime was there to make the message sink
in, I thought; and the violet kiss,
quavering and frail, all the way from Williamsburg, Iowa,
sealed some agreement we had for the next summer
as certain and relentless as time.

I didn't know this would be the last time.
If I had, I might even have prayed to Jesus
to let me see her once again next summer.
But how could I know she would sink,
her feet fat boats of cancer, in Williamsburg, Iowa,
alone, forsaken, without my last kiss?

I was ten, Jesus, and the idea of a kiss
at that time made my young stomach sink.
Let it be summer. Let it be Williamsburg, Iowa.

ALICE FULTON

Days through Starch and Bluing

(in memoriam: Catherine Callahan, "Katey," my grandmother)

Mondays sweating the flat smell
of boiled cloth, Octagon soap,
washday moves in. Stirring work-
clothes with a stick,
chafing grime against the washbcard's crimp,
labor-splurging to coddle the particular
Mrs. Westover's preference for blue and white paper-
ruled pinafores done just so, she knots
cubes of Rickett's bluing in small

knapsacks, swirls them through rinse water
till the tub mirrors a periwinkle winter
sky for her dingy whites.

Steam and lye.
The wringer chews things dry. Collars and cuffs
are dipped in the hot icing of starch.
Crisp wings, cups, crackable
as Willoware. She tacks the scraping
armfuls on five lines: shirts, bloomers,
livelier than when worn
doubledare the wind. They'll freeze soon enough,
her fingers are stiff as clothespins.
She sings a song. The sound forms quick clouds
that mark the time: "Take me out to the ball-
game, take me out to the . . ." After dark, she'll drag in
the tough sheets. They'll slit the snow toward home.

Tuesdays, uncurling linens,
towel-rolled, water-sprinkled
for slick ironing, she'll iron. Now she counts
her kids back from school. In the kitchen
they're spilling tea on their dresses.
Goodwhite. Proudblue. This happened
every week. She sits to think
of tonight's dinner. Tomorrow's pressing.

Grandma Chooses Her Plot at the County Cemetery

If it can't be out on the hill somewhere
I guess it'll have to be here.
I don't expect where really matters,
only not next to him, not close:
life was too hard for him,
he's soured the soil. Over by
that leaning oak would do, though
the shade won't count—sun, shade,
and shower won't matter then—
and digging them roots'll be hard.
Fine, I want them to suffer putting me down.
And you can find me better next to it,
if you've a mind to come here again
after I'm under and the hill's gone.
And I don't care what you say: you'll
sell that farm and never go back.
It never was nothing to any of you.
By that leaning oak will be just fine;
and make my box simply and cheap,
pine or gum if you can get it, never
liked them shiny steel things: God can't
get to you and you can't get out.
When he splits the sky with the judgment sound,
I want the busting out easy. I want
the coming up easier than the going down.

Moving

The house inside still looks like a house
but the blank rectangle of light
through the propped wide open front door
means emptiness. Inside, the slow men
move like mourners, noncommittal
among the labeled furniture, once decent
but today grown strangely shabby. Each table
is listed "scratched." In brightening
room to room, our pine-planked voices echo
as if they never spoke here before.

We watch moments of our lives move out
piece by piece through the front door
carelessly handled with care
by, for the moment, members of the family
(moving out, they move in
helplessly intimate, their big arms
touching our things, hauling
the weight of what we are).
We feel apologetic to be so heavy
and stand around like guests being served
saying, "Yes, that," and, "No, not that,"
watching decor become debris, and sunlight
sanding the floors already.

Note to the Previous Tenants

Thank you for leaving the bar of soap,
the roll of paper towels,
the sponge mop, the bucket.

I tried to scrub the white floor clean,
discovered it impossible,
and realized you had tried too.

Often, no doubt. The long hair in the sink
was a clue to what? Were you
boys or girls or what?

How often did you dance on the floor?
The place was broom clean. Your lives
were a great wind that has swept by.

Thank you; even the dirt
seemed a gift, a continuity
underlying the breaking of leases.

And the soap, green in veins
like meltable marble, and curved
like a bit of an ideal woman.

Lone, I took a bath with your soap
and had no towel not paper ones
and dried in the air like the floor.

The New House

This place is not ours:
the window sill refuses
to wear our drying wishbone
and the floors don't fit

the worn spot for carpets
we seem to take
everywhere we go.
The house still sings

its own tune, sending
our footsteps along the floor
through timbers that creak
to keep the basement washer

company, peopling that lair
of webs and laundry
where the furnace lifts
its arms to warm

the rooms. But the rooms
are cold, bent
on remembering
other hands caressing

woodwork with soft cloths
and feet that always
tiptoed. Wallpaper
has memorized
the places where
their pictures hung.
Soon enough, we know,
the rooms will give in.

Our own mice will shatter
cupboards and later
we will sprain our wrists
opening new bills.

But last night
windows threatened
to bring in the storm
and the back door banged

and banged, giving us
a message we could understand,
something menacing and wooden
that spoke, asking us to travel

to the storm's blind, silent eye.

Late, Passing Prairie Farm

All night like a star a single bulb
shines from the eave of the barn.
Light extends itself more and more
feebly into farther angles and overhead
into the trees. Where light ends
the world ends.

Someone left the light burning, but
the farm is alone. There is so much
silence that the house leans toward
the road. The last echo from dust
falling through floor joists happened
years ago.

Owls made a few dark lines across
that glow, but now the light has
erased all but itself—is now a pearl for
birds that move in the dark. They polish
this jewel by air from their wings. This glow
is their still dream.

The sill of the house is worn by
steps of travelers, gone—boards tell
their passage, their ending, copied
into the race. When you pass here, traveler,
you too can't keep from making sounds,
like theirs, that will last.

Incident

Charley Coleman told me this
how on his land used to be
a homestead cabin

         gone into prairie

how when a fellow came to see
the home he'd been a boy in
(in a station-wagon from some eastern state
with wife and kids and dog)
he led them in his pick-up several miles
through barbed-wire stock-fences
careful to refasten the gates

        Wyoming humanless
in all directions
I think it was around here someplace

how the light fled in the fellow's eyes
how the smile fell
how he turned without a word
followed him back to the highway

You Came as a Thought

when I was past such thinking
you came as a song when I had

finished singing you came when
the sun had just begun its set-

ting you were my evening star.

Sketch

Holding a picture up to the wall,
I look beyond your arms folded
and head cocked in appraisal to the window.
The wind's eye distinguishes nothing
out of the ordinary, but the leaves poise

like a nervous glade of bows before
the conductor dips his baton. All
our gestures begin their comforting
cadences again. Roasting smells
rise upstairs and linger.

Across the street a woman steps out
of her slack-spined house with a brood
of mottled cats, the same woman
who said to me—I don't know
where you've come from, Chicago

or wherever, but your dog has to be
on a leash. Now I realize that we
could have come here from anywhere,
not just the years we've lived together
listening in town after town to cars

accelerate uphill, trailing familiar
flags of music from their windows.
Perhaps this is only a way of ignoring
what was said about the leash,
but I think not. Standing together

watching sunset burnish a sliver of lake
hung in the leaves, we belong in our
life again. Dozens of windows flicker
in the valley. You seem to have just fallen
into my heart at its dusk.

HOWARD MOSS

The Meeting

It never occurred to me, never,
That you were attached to your universe,
Standing on a corner, waiting for a bus,
While the thought-trees grew above your head
And a meadow stretched its rambling sward
All the way up Fifth Avenue.
I was thinking of myself thinking of water,
Of how, each day I went about my job,
I missed one break in the Atlantic Ocean,
Of how I might have been here or there,
Fishing off the coast of Mexico,
Turning the sailboat round the bay,

Or, my chin resting on the concrete edge
Of a swimming pool, I could survey a hill,
The cows' soft blotches stranded in the grass.
Maybe it was that, that last green thing,
That led me into your deepening meadow,
That made me turn among the giant stones
To look one minute into your mind,
To see you running across a field,
The flowers springing up where you had touched.
It was there, I think, we finally met.

Waking, the Love Poem Sighs

I make myself wake early
In a rising light
So I can roll up on an elbow
To study you.
To get that image, that raw
Romantic thrill
The nucleus of the love poem
You claim I can not write,
The poem that has haunted me for
Years clogs like a plug in
Whatever canal feeds the fiery words
To my sub-vocalizing mind.

I am looking at you, full of waking
Wonder—ready to surprise you.
But nothing happens, except
A bird has awakened and the cat
Is home from stalking and looking
In the window at me. And you,
You breathe a sigh like you knew
I couldn't do it. That I could
Never wake early enough to pull the
Words out of this dream and make
Them work for me in daylight.

Rechargeable Dry Cell Poem

I used to love to lie awake past bedtime
reading by flashlight under the breathing covers.
Maybe that's why I take you to bed like a book now &
open you to a good place & turning
your pages quietly, love you to the end.
Explains why I'm Eveready, why
you're a strange new story every time.

My Love

when the crows fly away
with their compassion
and I remain to eat
whatever is left of my heart

I think of my love
with the odor of salt
of my love who holds me in her eyes
as if I were whole and beautiful

and I think of those
who walk the streets all night
frantic with desire and bruised
by the terrible small lips of rain

I touch you
as a blind man touches the dice
and finds he has won

BARTON SUTTER

Warmth

Sometimes want makes touch too much.
I hold my hands over your body
Like someone come in from the cold
Who takes off his clothes
And holds out his hands to the stove.

Scaffolding

Masons, when they start upon a building,
Are careful to test out the scaffolding;

Make sure that planks won't slip at busy points,
Secure all ladders, tighten bolted joints.

And yet all this comes down when the job's done
Showing off walls of sure and solid stone.

So if, my dear, there sometimes seem to be
Old bridges breaking between you and me

Never fear. We may let the scaffolds fall
Confident that we have built our wall.

The Anniversary

It was your smell that, for a day after, I carried with me.
My body smelled not of me but of you. The train
ticked over its crossings, stopped. In all its noises
I heard, suddenly and bewilderingly, your voice.

That was six years ago, the damp riverbank,
the Midwest storms massed, raining like an indictment,
the attacks of telephones, old interruptions talking.
Out of that, at your voice, I came to this different world.

Now, with the formal furniture, the black puppy quietly
lying at the door, the flames of the candles steady,
we are held by our reflections in the rose-colored wine—
a civilization of agreements, a closed place.

Thousands of miles away, the summer storms
still race in their green light. The night trains hurry on
across Canada, their noise empty of voices.
The old telephones busy themselves with the old words.

Here, in the Pacific evening, the puppy stands up
suddenly in the doorway and barks toward the dark street,
protecting what has come to include him. Six years, now.
I cannot tell his voice from the room's voice.

I cannot tell your voice from my own voice.

Past Love

I've come back
to these same old rooms
where the smell of new paint
and the rub of soft carpet
drown me
with memories of you.
Without even trying
I feel your touch,
warm artist's hand,
against my brown skin;
and without looking
I find your eyes
and that small half smile
that could win my heart.

You're my vagabond,
you're my lover,
and I see your face
through misty Sunday rains,
and I catch your eye
in the silver reflection
of my wine goblet.

PAUL ZIMMER

A Visit from Alphonse

Alphonse arrives as a fifth season
Of rain and wet snow,
Like something I had
Suffered a lifetime ago.

82

He is an incurable disease.
He talks of Wanda always,
All he remembers is Wanda,
When I had hidden her away,
Covered her like a sand grain
In the cool grey of my brain.

I have not lived for Wanda.
I am even able to forget her.
Except for the days
Her memory acts up like
A knee in bad weather or
When some self-indulgent pest
Like Alphonse comes back
And wakes the pain
That lies low in
The hollows of my chest.

WINFIELD TOWNLEY SCOTT

Brief Encounter

What I had never imagined: your return
In the guise of an actual girl: and there
She stood so slender in the summer light
And leaned—in such a way—the light came through
Her thin white shirt and silhouetted her
So I was shaken with remembering
And silent with impossible desire.
O I so heavy with years and all I knew,
All that she could not know—she was not you—

Yet shared (I thought) that vibrancy of silence,
Then walked to me and touched me, as if she knew
Something neither of us would ever say.

ALDEN NOWLAN

He Runs into an Old Acquaintance

"It's so good to talk with somebody
from the old neighborhood," she says.
It has been twenty years since we last met.

And now we exchange bits and pieces of the past,
whose tangible equivalent might be
the odds and ends I carry in my wallet,
a St. Jude's medal, old photographs taken
by a machine at a fair, membership cards,
and what-not; as happy with each other
as anybody would be who has found
a witness who can swear that he was where
he claims to have been. Then, too casually,
she says, "I missed you terribly at first."

To think she even noticed that I was gone!
Dear God, and to think I never once dreamt of asking
her to go walking with me by the river
or share in any of the other rites
performed by boys and girls when we were young.
She was so beautiful, is still, and I
stuttered when suddenly addressed by strangers,
couldn't carry a tune or dance or drive a car,
bumped my head constantly—a creature
part ape, part owl.

How could I know she saw
something in me I'd never seen in a mirror?

I ache with wishing I had touched her then.
What happened next wouldn't much matter now;
it would be all the same if we had only
looked at the water, hand-in-hand, just that
and nothing more, or if we had made love until
we had emptied ourselves in each other.

But it still matters that she'd not have laughed,
that she would have smiled and said, "Yes,"
if I had asked; and I didn't know.

DANA GIOIA

The Sunday News

Looking for something in the Sunday paper,
I flipped by accident through *Local Weddings*,
Yet missed the photograph until I saw
Your name among the headings.

And there you were, looking almost unchanged,
Your hair still long, though now long out of style,
And you still wore that stiff and serious look
You called a smile.

I felt as though we sat there face to face.
My stomach tightened. I read the item through.
It said too much about both families,
Too little about you.

Finished at last, I threw the paper down,
Stung by jealousy, my mind aflame,
Hating this man, this stranger whom you loved,
This printed name.

And yet I clipped it out to put away
Inside a book like something I might use,
A scrap I knew I wouldn't read again
Yet couldn't bear to lose.

MARK STRAND

For Her

Let it be anywhere
on any night you wish,
in your room that is empty and dark

or down the street
or at those dim frontiers
you barely see, barely dream of.

You will not feel desire,
nothing will warn you,
no sudden wind, no stillness of air.

She will appear,
looking like someone you knew:
the friend who wasted her life,

the girl who sat under the palm tree.
Her bracelets will glitter,
becoming the lights

of a village you turned from years ago.

Everything We Do

Everything we do is for our first loves
whom we have lost irrevocably
who have married insurance salesmen
and moved to Topeka
and never think of us at all.

We fly planes & design buildings
and write poems
that all say Sally I love you
I'll never love anyone else
Why didn't you know I was going to be a poet?

The walks to school, the kisses in the snow
gather, as we dream backwards, sweetness with age:
our legs are young again, our voices
strong and happy, we're not afraid.
We don't know enough to be afraid.

And now
we hold (hidden, hopeless) the hope
that some day
she may fly in our plane
enter our building read our poem

And that night, deep in her dream,
Sally, far in darkness, in Topeka,
with the salesman lying beside her,
will cry out
our unfamiliar name.

Sweetheart

Looking in a thicket
of forgotten papers, I find
a love letter of yours.
Seventeen years it's been
since I last thought of you.
Somewhere a perfect stranger
with your name nears forty,
like me, but these few words
show me all I want to know:
like locust skin, the shape
you had to leave behind
to grow away from here.

One Rose of Stone

Carved out of granite.

How can anyone believe that
or understand the patience
that caused a pair of hands
to painfully shape this flower
so perfectly, so carefully
then place this stone rose here
on this grave, just to mark a love?

Part Three

Quilt Song

for Alec Bond

A mist of snowflakes swirling in the street—
another blizzard? You've lost all track.
Astonished April waits somewhere
beyond the trees: not this week, not yet,
we'll test you for a few more days,
let your temper stretch itself another notch,
then give you floods—
just in case you thought you deserved better.

One more time you unfold
the old grandmother's quilt,
the one she called the Double Wedding Ring.
The child you once were
used it as a racetrack for tiny cars,
a kingdom home from school,
a comforter against most chills
and winds that still find all the cracks.

You walk the pattern one more time:
what you find is lost, and what
is lost remains, like an unfinished winter.
Warmed again, you wait
while snowflakes swirl in golden double loops.

Since You Seem Intent . . .

Since you seem intent on going away
to marry him (nor do I condone it)
I will list those memories which will stay
with me to partially atone for it:

the color of your eyes that afternoon
at Laguna Beach, which matched the ribbons in
your pigtails, matched the complexion
of the sky, the profound joy-sadness of the ocean;

I will remember you as one girl who
could drink any liquid in a bottle
faster than myself, a girl subtle
in saying yes, gentle in saying no.

I will remember how you worried
that your rosebud breasts were small,
in our old-fashioned room at the motel;
I will remember you as a girl who worried.

I will remember how you hated all
my favorite words, but came to tolerate them;
and how we mocked each other's ex-religions,
I, the Latinist; you, the bigot episcopal.

I will remember you as one I didn't want
to go, a girl I was just getting to know,
to whom, as day by day was lost, I couldn't
quite say: I do not want you to go.

The Departure

When you go away
you become everything I believe
you are, the steady light
from the lamps, warm
from a distance on my skin,
the piano still playing
somewhere in my mind, curtains
blowing at the window
speaking to me.

This Love

This love is a bruise
Discovered in the shower.

The day I met you I knew
What I was going to do:

Wear green to dramatize my eyes,
Combine silence and wit

In measures calculated
To make you suffer a bit.

Maybe even become
Your "secret sorrow."

I thought I could handle it.
Ten thousand proverbs

Couldn't have kept me
From digging this pit and falling in.

Serves me right that you're leaving.
Now let the pain I planned begin.

RICHARD TILLINGHAST

September: Last Day
at the Beach

A high blow tousled all the yachts
In the basin; green, yellow, and red shells
Bowled and whacked sides. The buoy bells
Scattered their moist petals into the air
And all up the beach the summer's gates
Were swinging shut. The wind smacked your hair

Onto your mouth, and all I now can see
Of your face is that you did not smile
At me. Even before the pale
Salt-wash flecked whitely at your ankles
Your name before my eyes ran grey.
I would not follow where the waves remold wrinkles

Of sand and drag the stem-eyed crabs
To dash on stones. I sat upon a dune
Watching you kilt up your skirts and frown
At the spray, thinking how after the dancing
And wine and kissing in taxicabs
You had come to me in the black of morning

Your damp hair braided like a child's,
Petal-sweet, and held with a rubber-band.
At rolls and coffee, when daybreak unwound
Us, we had talked awhile of staying over:
A walk on the beach would stay the pulls
Of plan, the tow of destination—
When we were two east-west trains in the station
Pulling apart, forever, forever.

MYRA SKLAREW

The Goodbye

This endsaying—moon pried loose
by grave force, pulled
out of earth's sweet atmosphere—
this has been formulated in every place.
In each text it is known.

At birth, the broken covenant
with before—parting from it hand
over hand along the dark way,
or valve closing
on its nine month work—breath
in the place of blood.

Or in sleep—it rises
like a ghostly glacier
bounded on each side
by consciousness;
it calls us
and we go at night
to that kindly absence—
sealed ark
bearing us toward morning.

Or in the sudden heat of love
when the body senses the cold deeply
like breathing in
The Goodbye—it is well known.
What more to say of it?

We play it back—old film,
refugees in our torn ships, sailing
the bruised distance.

We walk upright on this earth
for our allotted time. Love,
we pass you as before. Yet
this passing has the shape
of farewell.

JOHN SMITH

First, Goodbye

First, you will say goodbye. You will turn
   And for what you think is the last time gaze from the window
   To the bright and battering street headlong below.
Behind your eyes, your smile, the tears will burn.

You will not let them fall. You will stand
   As if you were a child or a cripple unable to walk.
   You will try though the words are like glass, you will try to talk,
But you will manage only a pathetic gesture of the hand.

All this is ordinary. You will be aware
   Of my presence behind you the world of our words away.
   And you will know, you will know there is nothing that I can say;
And then you will hear with your heart the dumbness of my despair

Articulate in the silence; it will cry
    Out in such a remonstrance of love that you will know
    No window or door or street may let you go,
Or your lips or my lips utter a last goodbye.

Absence

You have withdrawn,
receded into memory once again.
What was your presence I put away
like a carefully folded letter.

You stepped out of me
as out of a room, but the door is ajar;
through it I see the days ahead open
like a path to a sepulchre.

LINDA PASTAN

Dido's Farewell

The rain is chronic
at my windows, and candles drown
in their own wax.
Abandoned by light,
even the filaments of stars
go black. This afternoon
I propped your drenched roses
up on sticks,
they look like young girls
on crutches now.

You left
a partial map
of your right hand
on every doorknob,
and I follow from room
to room, nomad
in my own house,
my own heart knocking
at my ribs, demanding
to be let out.

❦

ELIZABETH JENNINGS

Thinking of Love

That desire is quite over
Or seems so as I lie
Using the sky as cover
And thinking of deep
Dreams unknown to a lover.

Being alone is now
Far from loneliness.
I can stretch and allow
Legs, arms, hands
Their complete freedom:
There is no-one to please.

But soon it comes—
Not simply the ache
Of a particular need,
But also the general hunger,
As if the flesh were a house
With too many empty rooms.

For a Friend

Late November, driving to Wichita.
A black veil of starlings
snags on a thicket and falls.
Shadows of wings skitter over
the highway, like leaves, like ashes.

You have been dead for six months;
though summer and fall
were lighter by one life,
they didn't seem to show it.
The seasons, those steady horses,
are used to the fickle weight
of our shifting load.

I'll guess how it was; on the road
through the wood, you stood up
in the back of the hangman's cart,
reached a low-hanging branch,
and swung up into the green leaves
of our memories.
                    Old friend,
the stars were shattered windshield glass
for weeks; we all were sorry.

They never found that part of you
that made you drink, that made you cruel.
You knew we loved you anyway.

Black streak across the centerline,
all highways make me think of you.

100

X, Oh X

The broken mirror.
The razor blade
still warm with
the whisper of
your life.

I will simply believe
you have gone
to live in another city.
Sometimes distant,
sometimes closer
than I will admit.

The fear of your
surrender, the
total closing up,
the fist of the mind
clenched tightly is
the prize I have
given you for travelling
so closely with me.

Beaver Moon—The Suicide of
a Friend

When somewhere life
breaks like a pane of glass,
and from every direction casual

voices are bringing you the news,
you say: I should have known.
You say: I should have been aware.
That last Friday he looked
so ill, like an old mountain-climber
lost on the white trails, listening
to the ice breaking upward, under
his worn-out shoes. You say:
I heard rumors of trouble, but after all
we all have that. You say:
what could I have done? and you go
with the rest, to bury him.
That night, you turn in your bed
to watch the moon rise, and once more
see what a small coin it is
against the darkness, and how everything else
is a mystery, and you know
nothing at all except
the moonlight is beautiful—
white rivers running together
along the bare boughs of the trees—
and somewhere, for someone, life
is becoming moment by moment
unbearable.

Moonlight

It will not hurt me when I am old,
  A running tide where moonlight burned
    Will not sting me like silver snakes;
The years will make me sad and cold,
  It is the happy heart that breaks.

The heart asks more than life can give,
  When that is learned, then all is learned;
    The waves break fold on jewelled fold,
But beauty itself is fugitive,
  It will not hurt me when I am old.

Warning

When I am an old woman I shall wear purple
With a red hat which doesn't go, and doesn't suit me,
And I shall spend my pension on brandy and summer gloves
And satin sandals, and say we've no money for butter.
I shall sit down on the pavement when I'm tired
And gobble up samples in shops and press alarm bells
And run my stick along the public railings
And make up for the sobriety of my youth.
I shall go out in my slippers in the rain
And pick the flowers in other people's gardens
And learn to spit.

You can wear terrible shirts and grow more fat
And eat three pounds of sausage at a go
Or only bread and pickle for a week
And hoard pens and pencils and beermats and things in boxes.

But now we must have clothes that keep us dry
And pay the rent and not swear in the street
And set a good example for the children.
We must have friends to dinner and read the papers.

But maybe I ought to practice a little now?
So people who know me are not too shocked and surprised
When suddenly I am old and start to wear purple.

RICHARD EBERHART

Hardy Perennial

In youth we dream of death,
In age we dream of life.

    I could not have cared less for life
    When young, employing savage pursuit
    Into the glories of the unknown,
    Fascinated by death's kingdom.

    The paradox was my brimming blood.
    My bright, my brimming blood, my force
    And power like a bridge to the future,
    Could not contain itself in white flesh.

In youth we dream of death,
In age we dream of life.

Now that death's savagery appears,
Each day nipping at my generation,
The hard facts of the world negate
Symbols of the mind striving otherwhere.

I would give love to every being alive,
Penetrating the secrets of living,
Discovering subtleties and profundities in
Any slightest gesture, or delicate glance.

STANLEY KUNITZ

I Dreamed That I Was Old

I dreamed that I was old: in stale declension
Fallen from my prime, when company
Was mine, cat-nimbleness, and green invention,
Before time took my leafy hours away.

My wisdom, ripe with body's ruin, found
Itself tart recompense for what was lost
In false exchange: since wisdom in the ground
Has no apocalypse or pentecost.

I wept for my youth, sweet passionate young thought,
And cozy women dead that by my side
Once lay: I wept with bitter longing, not
Remembering how in my youth I cried.

Ago

Old.
Few years more attend me, I am redundant
A useless tool, a broken body, seedless.
Look at me and you see a season regretting.

I foresaw this once
But it was not like this. I saw
An age of goodness, of gifts spent out and needed.
Age is a going back.

Is a kind of return,
To the breast, the womb, the mother.
I do without all and face the winter regretting.
The child in me who can play no longer.

Blue Springs, Georgia

On the New Jersey shore he met her
when he took leave from the sub
to explore Yankees and their cool blood.
He dubbed her Jenny, though it wasn't
her name. Stubborn woman, he'd croon,
like a jenny ass. They married when
the war was done. Carried her back

to the warm Georgia sun where vine-held
shacks pocked the fields. Creases formed
around her snow-cold eyes, pale skin
browned. She learned to fry fatback, make
cornbread with fine white meal, knew his
fingers, green from pecan husks. She ate,
spoke, lived with his Southern accent.

But sometimes her cornbread baked sweet,
bright yellow. Sometimes her words rang
crisp, hard as a Jersey winter. And she
gave him no sons for the land, no daughters
to breed grandsons for the land. That's
what happens, they said. Eula Hawkins-
that-was-Bridgers has *five* boys, they said.

Remember Eula, that gal you once courted?
Five boys, they said, and all you got
is a bitter damn pill to swallow. So,
he swallowed, poured his red clay sweat
on the fields, his bitterness into her.
The farm swelled. She grew stringy, aged
odd, fed wrens she called her "babies."

He left her the right to live in the house,
but the land, the heavy pecan trees,
slash pines, the sleek, fat land he left
in his family. His brother's boys visit
her, listen to her brittle bones, tend
her needs, keep guard on their land, and
watch the snowflakes fall in her eyes.

The Belly Dancer in the
Nursing Home

The crazy ladies are singing again,
clapping their hands and gums to the music,
dancing their wheelchairs to and fro
with a frail and bony toe.
In the front row, some old men,
flushed with the heat of the season,
are thumping their tuneless canes and stumps,
driving old age and infirmity
out of the room like an unwanted guest.
Meanwhile, the belly dancer,
all sweat and sequins, muscles and skin,
ripples and pumps,
her skimpy metallic costume slipping
beneath her secret hair,
until even my father, slumped in his chair,
lifts his voice and quickens:
Goddamn! he sings. Look there!
Until we're all dancing and singing,
hips, breasts, and heads ringing
the immodest, unlikely air,
until the performance is over.
The women stiffen into their chairs;
the men lean back on their silence;
and my father folds up as in prayer,
with just enough breath left to whisper.
And sing. And dance. And swear.

Jane Seagrim's Party

This calls for a toast. She hates
To admit it, but Jane is one hundred today
And reporters are coming by to watch
Her blow the candles out and ask,
Dearie, how, how did you do it
And how can we, who love speed,
Drink, cigars and have so deep
A sense of the tragic? And she will grin,
Exposing blackness on either side
Of her original stumpy canines and maybe
Wink who laid out three good husbands,
Receives post cards from her kids' kids
Having fun in another world
With people in it, can't even follow
TV to see the good life
In color—like two weeks in Hawaii—
She's missed, and is terrified of children
Who want, hugging, to break her bones,
Eats mush and drinks tea, thank you,
Won't be sampling her own cake,
And anyway the taste buds have all bloomed
And died long ago and it's shocking
To sit on the toilet and look down.

Nevertheless, one joy is left—
To pull, if she had it, from under her skirts,
A dainty pistol out and, right
In the middle of their disbelief,
Shoot these smartasses dead
Who thought this old life
Had no more to show them.

In the Basement of the Goodwill Store

In musty light, in the thin brown air
of damp carpet, doll heads and rust,
beneath long rows of sharp footfalls
like nails in a lid, an old man stands
trying on glasses, lifting each pair
from the box like a glittering fish
and holding it up to the light
of a dirty bulb. Near him, a heap
of enameled pans as white as skulls
looms in the catacomb shadows,
and old toilets with dry red throats
cough up bouquets of curtain rods.

You've seen him somewhere before.
He's wearing the green leisure suit
you threw out with the garbage,
and the Christmas tie you hated,
and the ventilated wingtip shoes
you found in your father's closet
and wore as a joke. And the glasses
which finally fit him, through which
he looks to see you looking back—
two mirrors which flash and glance—
are those through which one day
you too will look down over the years,
when you have grown old and thin
and no longer particular,
and the things you once thought
you were rid of forever
have taken you back in their arms.

Old Clothes

How could you not keep them—
which grew the better for wear

which you saw through that work
under the car, that deep turf
you spaded, that clinging cold
of the stream, and now

which still return as friends
in whispers of mothballs
and summers at the lake
to forgive you once more
your merely human shape?

Song for a Departure

Could you indeed come lightly
Leaving no mark at all
Even of footsteps, briefly
Visit not change the air
Of this or the other room,
Have quick words with us yet be
Calm and unhurried here?

So that we should not need—
When you departed lightly
Even as swift as coming
Letting no shadow fall—
Changes, surrenders, fear,
Speeches grave to the last,
But feel no loss at all?

Lightest things in the mind
Go deep at last and can never
Be planned or weighed or lightly
Considered or set apart.
Then come like a great procession,
Touch hours with drums and flutes:
Fill all the rooms of our houses
And haunt them when you depart.

Call Them Back

Whatever it is you're missing, whatever
the whys of your needs, what things you painted over
or had hauled away in dusty trucks, covered, the way
the ugly smoke covers that magnificently stretched sky,
whatever loved you and let you go, your heart left to float,
and shiver, and explode finally at the slightest touch,
whatever you felt,
especially
whatever you felt, old smells and tastes, the fast beauty
of the city, and there's no explaining it,
metal spirits of the century honking in your sleep, filling
the cold spaces with sound, the dead magicians, dead musicians
with no eyes, no hands, but who breathe in your ear
like lovers, even from so far away,
the dead musicians who put me back together
when I was alone and broke,
birth songs, love songs, god songs,
call them back,
call them back and listen, that they might make sense
of your boiling insides, feelings you misplaced
among the meat shelves, call them now
whatever it is you're looking for, motherghosts or fatherghosts,
all the ghosts, why don't you call them home?

Return

August sun hangs low above the city,
dusty clouds unwavering
as if to hold you here.
You called these "dog days" once,
not knowing why, and when it was too hot
you'd sleepwalk up and down the streets
lingering at each window
for what you hoped would happen,
though it never did.

And now you must return,
renewing claims on what you've lost—
with nothing to show you lived here
but a small synapse behind your eyes,
an out of focus photograph
in albums never kept,
the old neighbor lady who's remained
through all the intervening years—
near death now, she accepts
the child who never left.

🌿

Looking Both Ways

for Don and Connie

Old leaves, the perfume of moldering,
dirt beneath my nails.
I want to empty all my pockets.

114

This is my house to sweep.
Even the crumbs in the corner
belong to me.

In this closet
for each velvet dress on a hanger
at least one night danced.

All these glasses poured wine.
These dusty dishes
sat on lace and linen tables.

All night back and forth
over a street light's glare
the curtain swings.

Somewhere a door must be fanning the air,
someone practicing an exit,
a girl looking both ways.

❦

KEITH WILSON

A Prayer for Rivers

I live in the twilight of my vices,
old winds that blow across my face.

I know the stillness of the night.
I walk, the rivers are bright with moon.
Wrapping my coat about my neck, I pray,
to whatever gods, that night leaves me
not alone, but full, drifting down this street,
this time, you completely beside me,
riverfrost on your hair, and on mine.

❦

Great Things Have Happened

We were talking about the great things
that have happened in our lifetimes;
and I said, "Oh, I suppose the moon landing
was the greatest thing that has happened
in my time." But, of course, we were all lying.
The truth is the moon landing didn't mean
one-tenth as much to me as one night in 1963
when we lived in a three-room flat in what once
    had been
the mansion of some Victorian merchant prince
(our kitchen had been a clothes closet, I'm sure),
on a street where by now nobody lived
who could afford to live anywhere else.
That night, the three of us, Claudine, Johnnie and me,
woke up at half-past four in the morning
and ate cinnamon toast together.

"Is that all?" I hear somebody ask.

Oh, but we were silly with sleepiness
and, under our windows, the street-cleaners
were working their machines and conversing in
    Italian, and
everything was strange without being threatening,
even the tea-kettle whistled differently
than in the daytime: it was like the feeling
you get sometimes in a country you've never visited
before, when the bread doesn't taste quite the same,
the butter is a small adventure, and they put
paprika on the table instead of pepper,
except that there was nobody in this country
except the three of us, half-tipsy with the wonder
of being alive, and wholly enveloped in love.

Some Night Again

When the world vanishes, I will come back
here by the power of my dreams and create it
again, starting where that clear
depth in the mountain lake began,
where you swam one night across the moonlight
and I thought: Still, it's good, though it has to end.

Tomorrow

Your best friend is gone,
your other friend, too.
Now the dream that used to turn in your sleep,
sails into the year's coldest night.

What did you say?
Or was it something you did?
It makes no difference—the house of breath collapsing
around your voice, your voice burning, are nothing to worry about.

Tomorrow your friends will come back;
your moist open mouth will bloom in the glass of storefronts.
Yes. Yes. Tomorrow they will come back and you
will invent an ending that comes out right.

Waiting

As in a thunderstorm at night,
pulsing lamplight brightens and dims;

wind gusts, at the window, sharpen
the odor of old geraniums;

the bronze bowl hardens its sheen; the cat's
ribs ripple, shuddering his tail;

thrust up from sleep, the children
peer from their rooms, wondering

where they have been: it has come to this
as the warp of your shadow enters my mind,

as I promise again I will wait here
for the rain, for you, to arrive.

Part Four

Julian Barely Misses
Zimmer's Brains

The end of winter seeped up
through our boots.
                    Julian and I
Were hunting over the fields
For the things that splayed
The deep, confident tracks in
The final snow, when Julian
Slipped on a viscid clod
And his shotgun cracked
Both barrels past my ear.

My God, my God, I see it yet!

I sit down on a cold stone
And feel my chubby brains
Float down like stuffing from
Old cushions, I feel my face
Rammed back through the grinder
Of my teeth and birds
Returning to fork me apart
Like tender meat.

Yet I am alive to tell you that
Ducks applauded overhead and game
Flicked all about, but Julian
And I had enough of shooting.

Now the only heavy footprints in
The snow are ours.
                    Spring
Has come and I am alive
With the sense that I am still alive.

A Story That Could Be True

If you were exchanged in the cradle and
your real mother died
without ever telling the story
then no one knows your name,
and somewhere in the world
your father is lost and needs you
but you are far away.

He can never find
how true you are, how ready.
When the great wind comes
and the robberies of the rain
you stand on the corner shivering.
The people who go by—
you wonder at their calm.

They miss the whisper that runs
any day in your mind,
"Who are you really, wanderer?"—
and the answer you have to give
no matter how dark and cold
the world around you is:
"Maybe I'm a king."

H. R. COURSEN

Suburban

People did die in our neighborhood
when I was young. In 1939 alone,
Eddie McIntyre, who lived next door,

fell off a mountain in New Hampshire,
and Mr. Whitehead, who lived on the
other side of us, had a stroke
while he was shaving and died
in his bathroom. And Mrs. Haynes—
she wore a lot of makeup
and looked like a clown
with her rouged cheeks, and she
had a smile that one recognized
as desperate, in retrospect. She had
no children, and she always seemed
to want to hug us as we walked past
her house to school. I wonder—
if we had let her hug us—whether
Mrs. Haynes would have hanged herself
early one morning, while
we passed by to school.

Reading Room, the New York Public Library

In the reading room in the New York Public Library
All sorts of souls were bent over silence reading the past,
Or the present, or maybe it was the future, persons
Devoted to silence and the flowering of the imagination,
When all of a sudden I saw my love.
She was a faun with light steps and brilliant eye
And she came walking among the tables and rows of persons,

Straight from the forest to the center of New York,
And nobody noticed, or raised an eyelash.
These were fixed on imaginary splendors of the past,
Or of the present, or maybe of the future, maybe
Something as seductive as the aquiline nose
Of Eleanor of Aquitaine, or Cleopatra's wrist-locket in Egypt,
Or maybe they were thinking of Juliana of Norwich.

The people of this world pay no attention to the fauns
Whether of this world or of another, but there she was,
All gaudy pelt, and sleek, gracefully moving,
Her amber eye was bright among the porticoes,
Her delicate ears were raised to hear of love,
Her lips had the appearance of green grass
About to be trodden, and her shanks were smooth and sleek.

Everybody was in the splendor of his imagination,
Nobody paid any attention to this splendor
Appearing in the New York Public Library,
Their eyes were on China, India, Arabia, or the Balearics,
While my faun was walking among the tables and eyes
Inventing their world of life, invisible and light,
In silence and sweet temper, loving the world.

The Lost Carnival

1.

She feels her presence as never
before, here where the dim little carnival
departs. Where she is never
following, never, never.

The young girl stands at the circle of beaten ground.
Sparrows and starlings peckpecking
the stale confetti bits of popcorn.
On the power pole crossbar
a big crow hunches his shoulders.

2.

She remembers. The shouts of brass, the glory
of festoons, the candy butcher's red tattoo,
AMERICA. But nothing can be sadder
than the carousel zebra's chipped nose.
How the Ferris wheel rattled its gondolas in wind.

3.

Where has the little carnival gone?
She imagines a rocky mountain pass, the
elephants trumpeting in the blizzard, the acrobats
shouldering the mired wagons. Tigers
pad soft and restless through the falling flakes.

On Certain Mornings
Everything Is Sensual

At breakfast
Veiled dancers
Rose from my coffee cup;

When I opened the door,
Summer smothered me
With kisses;

On my way to work,
An old Cadillac revved past,
Fins flared
Like passionate nostrils;

And now I hardly dare
Press the button
On the water-cooler.

What can I do?
It's been like this all day.
Even the alarm clock
Had its hands all over me.

Poem for People Who Are Understandably Too Busy to Read Poetry

Relax. This won't last long.
Or if it does, or if the lines
make you sleepy or bored,
give in to sleep, turn on
the T.V., deal the cards.
This poem is built to withstand
such things. Its feelings
cannot be hurt. They exist
somewhere in the poet,
and I am far away.
Pick it up any time. Start it
in the middle if you wish.
It is as approachable as melodrama,
and can offer you violence
if it is violence you like. Look,
there's a man on a sidewalk;
the way his leg is quivering
he'll never be the same again.
This is your poem
and I know you're busy at the office
or the kids are into your last good nerve.
Maybe it's sex you've always wanted.
Well, *they lie together*
like the party's unbuttoned coats,
slumped on the bed
waiting for drunken arms to move them.
I don't think you want me to go on;
everyone has his expectations, but this
is a poem for the entire family.
Right now, Budweiser

is dripping from a waterfall,
deodorants are hissing into armpits
of people you resemble,
and *the two lovers are dressing now,*
saying farewell.
I don't know what music this poem
can come up with, but clearly
it's needed. For it's apparent
they will never see each other again
and we need music for this
because there was never music when he or she
left *you* standing on that corner.
You see, I want this poem to be nicer
than life. I want you to look at it
when anxiety zigzags your stomach
and the last tranquilizer is gone
and you need someone to tell you
I'll be here when you want me
like the sound inside a shell.
The poem is saying that to you now.
But don't give up anything for this poem.
It doesn't expect much. It will never say more
than listening can explain.
Just keep it in your attache case
or in your house. And if you're not asleep
by now, or bored beyond sense,
the poem wants you to laugh. Laugh at
yourself, laugh at this poem, at all poetry.
Come on:

Good. Now here's what poetry can do.
Imagine yourself a caterpillar.
There's an awful shrug and, suddenly,
you're beautiful for as long as you live.

The Poem You Asked For

My poem would eat nothing.
I tried giving it water
but it said no,

worrying me.
Day after day,
I held it up to the light,

turning it over,
but it only pressed its lips
more tightly together.

It grew sullen, like a toad
through with being teased.
I offered it all my money,

my clothes, my car with a full tank.
But the poem stared at the floor.
Finally I cupped it in

my hands, and carried it gently
out into the soft air, into the
evening traffic, wondering how

to end things between us.
For now it had begun breathing,
putting on more and

more hard rings of flesh.
And the poem demanded the food,
it drank up all the water,

beat me and took my money,
tore the faded clothes
off my back,

said Shit,
and walked slowly away,
slicking its hair down.

Said it was going
over to your place.

PETER DAVISON

The Poem in the Park

She waited eagerly on a park bench,
holding in her arms the humming of the day,
her eyes welling with *lacrimae rerum*.
I walked toward her through the bricky streets
tasting as I came the sky of the public park,
its gates ajar, its paths cast wide in welcome,
the bench warm beside her
with the words the poem and I would engage together.
But as I walked in under the sighing trees,
a gust of wind scattered from the dark pond
a flock of mallards, wings whistling,
crying out and fanning toward the harbor
over the buildings between the park and the sea.

Not till hours later, hemmed in between
office telephone and office typewriter,
did it come back to me. I'd left the poem
seated motionless upon a wooden bench
with tears in its eyes.

To Build a Poem

Building a poem is like building a house
where raw material, pointed word and nail,
are laid out—in piles, and mixed without a rule,
two-by-fours stacked in readiness for the saw,
and words anticipate order, in order to beam
the page as nails await the hammer.

Then I hear the sounds start to form and the hammer
whangs and bangs the sill down to ground the house
in a form which will hold every rafter and beam
in place. And the poem takes shape as I nail
my thoughts and stud the page with images I saw
while framing a closet, not in the book of rules.

In my house I rule
out all excess lines, and simplify as I hammer
on the plate with sixteen-penny nails, and saw
the rafters, one by one, careful not to cut too much as I house
possibility with walls and roof. A fingernail
of a moon shines on the skeleton of frame and beams

light on a poem in my mind and I beam
to think of a couplet or a slant rhyme that will fit the rule
of a sonnet or sestina just like the beveled banisters I nail
to the stairs. I hear the singing of those hammer
sounds, like words that leap to dance as they house
the music of the poem, an up-down cadence like the song of the
  saw.

Now the finish work is tricky because the see-saw
of a bad rhyme or extra foot must be chiseled away. Every nail
must be set in the woodwork and the house
should be tight, and the kitchen cabinet drawers more exact than
   rule
of thumb. But in the polishing of a poem, a quiet Jim Beam
sometimes helps during the final hammering.

And who will live in this space built by a sixteen-oz. hammer
and days of hefting and fitting? It is a house
for me to dance in, and sleep in and hang the print of the Matisse I
   saw
at the Metropolitan. I will not live by the rule
here in this house where poems are waiting to grow and beam
like the prism I hung in my window by one small nail.

I know that when night slips in quietly, and the old fingernail
of a moon I saw scrapes across the blue-black sky, darkness will not
   rule
my hammering heart because I shall let the poem out of my house
   and it will beam.

CARL CONOVER

Nude Reclining at Word Processor, in Pastel

She carefully regards her software. The amber
light pulses along her thighs as she searches
in vast undocumented libraries, without rotundas,
for the mere appearance of desire, catalogued
long ago, now concealed with her archives.
These are the old landscapes of her sighs.

She ties a carbon ribbon in her hair and dreams,
longing for the missing text and the hard copy.

MICHAEL BLUMENTHAL

Back from the Word Processing Course, I Say to My Old Typewriter

Old friend, you
who were once in the avant-garde,
you of the thick cord
and the battered plug,
the slow and deliberate characters
proportionally spaced, shall we
go on together as before?
Shall we remain married
out of the cold dittos of conviction
and habit? Or should we move on
to some new technology of ease
and embellishment—Should I run off
with her, so much like you when
you were young, my aged Puella
of the battered keys, so lovely
in that bleached light of the first morning?

Old horse,
what will it be like
when the next young filly
comes along? How will I love you,
crate of my practiced strokes,
when she cries out: *new new*
and asks me to dance again?

Oh plow for now, old boat,
through these familiar waters,
make the tides come in
once more! Concubined love,
take me again into your easy arms,
make this page wild once more
like a lustful sheet! Be wet,
sweet toy, with your old ink:
vibrate those aging hips again
beneath these trembling hands.

ROY SCHEELE

Dancer

How can it be,
she wonders, her heart
goes out to it still,
the single tree out back?
Its apples never came
to much; nevertheless
it goes on bearing,
if only to sweeten the grass.

Some days it's been
a comfort to her.
A mist of buds in spring,
and then the long-drawn
whitening, the petals
poured full of light
much in the way the dancers' skirts

dazzle the eyes
in Degas' paintings.
A dancer, yes: she sees
herself, long-legged girl
of long ago, her skin as pale
as apple flesh, whirling
around in the yard,
making her long dress swirl.

PAUL B. JANECZKO

This poem is for Nadine

who bends in garden rows
with straw hat
sunny back
flowered skirt
gathered in one hand
while the other
yanks
tosses weeds
toward dented white enamel pot;

who scolds greedy pennyroyal
comforts lavender
pinches rosemary and rue
with shears snips
cosmos foxglove delphinium
while our striped cat suns
in day lilies;

who this snowy night
rubs her small hands
wishing them lined with earth.

🌿

137

On Addy Road

A flicker with a broken neck
we found on the road, brought home, and laid
under a beech tree, liver-red the leaves.

On gaming-table green, in autumn shade,
we spread his yellow-shafted wing;
the spokes slid closed when we let go.

Splendid as the king
of spades, black half-moon under chin,
breast of speckled ermine,

scarlet ribbon at the nape—
how long before his raiment fade,
and gold slats tear within the cape?

We left him on the chilly grass.
Through the equinoctial night
we slept and dreamed

of the wetland meadow where,
one tawny dawn, the red fox crept—
an instant only, then his pelt

merged with the windbent reeds,
not to be seen again.
Next morning, going barefoot to the lawn,

we found the flicker's body gone, and saw
in the dew of the sandy road
faint print of a fox's paw.

Walking with Your Eyes Shut

Your ears receive a platter of sound
heaped where you are, in the center, verging
off at far edges that move as you pass,
like a great hoopskirt of listening through the world.
A brick wall compresses your right ear's horizon
on that side, but the whole sound sky balloons
again all around. A cardinal's whistle
soars up and arcs down behind you. A bluejay
unrolls its part of the day, a long streamer over you,
and then little discs receding smaller and
smaller into the infinity that lives
in the middle of the woods beyond. You carry
this dome all the time. Today you know it,
a great rich room, a musical sky.

Markers

1.
The pear tree, more dead than alive,
bears nothing but the sky
that ripens in its limbs.

2.
The leaves falling around me
like scales
from my eyes. The stretch of clouds
like thin shells
that help me know
how far the sky goes.

3.
Sometimes the steel light of early morning
sometimes the wine light of evening.
For one second I love the streetlight
circled now only
by moths of snow.

PAUL ZIMMER

Rollo's Miracle

Rollo says, "I can bring down rain."
We say, "Bull crap!" and slug him
On his bicep. But he says,
"Underwear ain't fit to wear!"
And lightning cracks its knuckles,
Thunder pulls the plug out.
Fish could swim in what comes down.

When it lets up we say to Rollo,
"Bull crap, buddy, you got lucky!"
But Wanda is giving Rollo the eye.

"Underwear ain't fit to wear!"
He chants again and the clouds
Uncork, the river starts to rise.
Wanda takes Rollo by the arm,
They go off to meet the rainbow.

We stand there with the cold rain
Sighing in our socks. Cecil says,
"Underwear ain't fit to wear."

"Underwear ain't fit to wear!"
Shouts Zimmer. Lester whispers,
"Underwear ain't fit to wear."
But that sun shines on and on—
Bright as a fresh dropped egg.

LAURA VALAITIS

A Field Poem

things remember me.
a feather leads me
to the black bird overhead,
a weed points me
towards the lone eucalyptus tree.

I sit there for hours
inside the world of the high grass.
the ears of all my bodies open
and I hear the wind
that carries this life so joyously,
just like the ocean
carries the light on its back
for miles and miles and miles.

The One to Grieve

anyone could hunt the old dog
but the old man loved him most
talked to him as he would a child
brought home sweets from town
but could not follow him in rough terrain

the old man died first
& the dog looked for him
along the creek
in the flat woods
he sniffed the road which led to town
and walked to church on Sunday alone

anyone could hunt the old dog
if they could find him after that.

A Dog in San Francisco

Sitting in an empty house
with a dog from the Mexican Circus!
O Daisy, embrace is my only pleasure.
Holding and hugging my friends. Education.
A wave of eucalyptus. Warm granite.
These are the things I have in my heart.
Heart and skills, there's nothing else.

I usually don't like small dogs but you
like midwestern women take over the air.
You leap into the air and pivot
a diver going up! You are known
to open the fridge and eat when you wish
you can roll down car windows and step out
you know when to get off the elevator.

I always wanted to be a dog
but I hesitated
for I thought they lacked certain skills.
Now I want to be a dog.

SAMUEL EXLER

The Cats

The cats have gone off to hunt. Last winter
They were human, dozing beside the woodstove,
Rubbing against my leg, yawning, stretching,
Claws nicking the carpet.
But they no longer answer my call
To come in at night. They are gone
And stay away for days.
Something wild has entered into them
That is the dark, that is
Not us, that is what they were like
Before we agreed to be friends.

Driving through Coal Country
in Pennsylvania,

sometimes you come on a whole
valley that's one gray excavation.
Each valley saddens me.
It's like seeing someone you know
but can hardly recognize anymore,
scarred up, shaved, sick
from a long operation,
only the operation's still going on,
and there are no doctors—
just dump trucks in the distance
raising dust.

For Richard Chase

Looking like all outdoors
the old tale-teller from the mountains
enters a highschool classroom in California.

He is himself a mountain:
his face has the lay of coves and hollows.
His shoulders heave up like rock-backed ridges,
His eyes sail and hover like hunting hawks.
Shimmering in his mind like mountain springs,
stories trickle off his tongue, fall
fast, then flow.

Riddles tumble down the stream of his speaking,
gold in gravel.
Even his silences glitter
like streaks of mica in gray rock.

From a knapsack of wonders
the old man takes a seashell.
He holds it to a student's ear and asks:
"What do you hear?"

The student thinks the old man
would make a nice poster
for his bedroom wall
which already has stars
painted on the ceiling.
He listens to the shell and says:
"The freeway?"

Conquerors

By sundown we came to a hidden village
Where all the air was still
And no sound met our tired ears, save
For the sorry drip of rain from blackened trees
And the melancholy song of swinging gates.
Then through a broken pane some of us saw
A dead bird in a rusting cage, still
Pressing his thin tattered breast against the bars,
His beak wide open. And
As we hurried through the weed-grown street,
A gaunt dog started up from some dark place
And shambled off on legs as thin as sticks
Into the wood, to die at least in peace.
No-one had told us victory was like this;
Not one amongst us would have eaten bread
Before he'd filled the mouth of the grey child
That sprawled, stiff as a stone, before the shattered door.
There was not one who did not think of home.

The Soldiers Returning

it was almost easy to say goodby
we said it we kept saying it *goodby*
goodby no one was listening

we travelled
pretending we were pursued by something good
in spite of empty horizons

we stood on the parapets of distant hunger
and slept in strange beds
in the red-light districts of the impotent

sometimes we knew
what we were doing and did it
sometimes we were not sure

now we return as the white hand
returns to its glove
and how to convince the darkness we are here
when it has so many others to care for

we return bearing the secret
that there is no secret
no collusion no plot
wars occur because men want them
and peace occurs when they are tired

we who were hired to kill
but not by anyone we could name
not by anyone we could talk to about it
return to the terrible menace of love
and to our children

PHILIP DACEY

The Amputee Soldier

Look at me move
My one, good hand.
I will conjure with it.

I will make
Another hand, as powerful,
And take it for my own.

With that new hand,
I will make signs
In the air. Even I

Shall not understand them.

Winter Twilight

Over the dark highway
over the woods
and the clusters of small houses,
the clouds appear

The great clouds of a winter twilight!

When I see them I feel like a hundred men
who know they have slipped out of prison
without a trace.

JONATHAN HOLDEN

Full Moon, Rising

So low it used to seem almost
perverse, like the risen dome of some dead
city, the full moon, rising, might have been
an omen—a public event
looming so great all roads would lead to it.
Whichever way I'd turn
on the small playground
I could not avoid it,
I'd find myself walking toward the moon,
though it is long since, now, that I have learned
what the full moon portends—
nothing, except that when you notice it
you're apt to be alone.
A name, someone you still love, comes to mind.

You remember, just then, that the earth is turning,
and feel, for a moment, certain
that as you notice it
you are the only one.

At Midnight

Somewhere in the night,
a dog is barking,
starlight like beads of dew
along his tight chain.
No one is there
beyond the dark garden,
nothing to bark at
except, perhaps, the thoughts
of some old man
sending his memories
out for a midnight walk,
a rich cape
woven of many loves
swept recklessly
about his shoulders.

While every effort has been made to secure permission, it has in a few cases proved impossible to trace the author or author's executor. Permission to reprint copyrighted poems is gratefully acknowledged to the following:

ALICE JAMES POETRY COOPERATIVE, for "Absence" by Elizabeth Knies from *Threesome Poems* published by Alice James Books, Copyright © 1976 by Elizabeth Knies.

AMPERSAND PRESS, for "Laughing Backwards," Copyright © by Jim Hall (first appeared in *Ham Operator* published by Ampersand Press).

ANDREW MOUNTAIN PRESS, Hartford, CT, and APPALACHIAN JOURNAL, for "My Grandfather in Search of Moonshine" by George Ella Lyon, Copyright © 1983 by Andrew Mountain Press.

ATHENEUM PUBLISHERS, INC., for "The Poem in the Park" from *A Voice in the Mountain*, Copyright © 1977 by Peter Davison; "The Meeting" from *Selected Poems*, Copyright © 1971 by Howard Moss; and "For Her" and "Tomorrow" from *Selected Poems*, Copyright © 1980 by Mark Strand.

THE BEST CELLAR PRESS, for "X, Oh X" by Mark Simpson from *Forty Nebraska Poets*, Copyright © by Greg Kuzma, The Best Celler Press.

BOA EDITIONS, LTD., for "Warmth" from *Cedarhome*, Copyright © 1977 by Barton Sutter.

GEORGE BOGIN, for "Abraham" (first appeared in *Poetry East*), Copyright © 1983 by George Bogin.

CARNEGIE MELLON UNIVERSITY PRESS, for "Poem for People Who Are Understandably Too Busy to Read Poetry" from *Work and Love*, Copyright © 1981 by Stephen Dunn and "Waking, the Love Poem Sighs" from *The Lady from the Dark . . .*, Copyright © 1977 by Jim Hall.

THE ESTATE OF JOHN CIARDI, for "On Being Much Better Than Most and Yet Not Quite Good Enough" by John Ciardi, published by Rutgers University Press.

THE COACH HOUSE PRESS, Toronto, for the Canadian rights to "A Dog in San Francisco" and "To a Sad Daughter" from *Secular Love* by Michael Ondaatje, Copyright © 1984 by The Coach House Press.

COMMONWEAL, for "One-Night Fair" by Nancy Price, published in *Commonweal*, Copyright © 1966 by Commonweal Foundation.

H. R. COURSEN, for "Suburban," published in *Hope Farm* (Cider Mill Press, Stratford, CT, 1979).

PHILLIP DACEY, for "The Amputee Soldier," Copyright © 1977 by Phil

154

155

Bishop, Elizabeth, 60
Blumenthal, Michael, 135
Bogin, George, 46
Chappell, Fred, 127
Ciardi, John, 26
Conover, Carl, 134
Coursen, H. R., 124
Dacey, Philip, 147
Davison, Peter, 132
Dickey, William, 80
Driscoll, Jack, 49
Dunn, Stephen, 129
Eberhart, Richard, 104, 126
Evans, David Allan, 12
Exler, Samuel, 143
Farnsworth, Robert, 74
Folk, Pat, 17
Fried, Elliot, 26
Fulton, Alice, 65
Gioia, Dana, 85
Giovanni, Nikki, 10
Hall, Jim, 29, 77
Hathaway, James B., 19
Hazo, Samuel, 9, 22
Heaney, Seamus, 80
Hemp, Christine E., 133
Hemschemeyer, Judith, 93
Hey, Phil, 88, 111
Holden, Jonathan, 11, 144, 149
Huddle, David, 51, 61
Janeczko, Paul B., 137
Jauss, David, 128
Jennings, Elizabeth, 44, 99, 106, 112
Johnson, Don, 24
Joseph, Jenny, 103

Keiter, Anne, 82
Kinnell, Galway, 34
Knies, Elizabeth, 98
Kooser, Ted, 24, 45, 100, 110, 151
Kopp, Karl, 73
Kunitz, Stanley, 12, 105
LaBombard, Joan, 38
Laughlin, J., 74
Levis, Larry, 131
Lipsitz, Lou, 149
Locklin, Gerald, 92
Lyon, George Ella, 50, 62
Meinke, Peter, 1, 87
Miller, Jim Wayne, 6, 33, 78, 144
Moss, Howard, 75
Nathan, Leonard, 109
Nelms, Sheryl L., 7
Nowlan, Alden, 20, 84, 116
Oliver, Mary, 101
Ondaatje, Michael, 39, 142
Orlen, Steve, 36
Pack, Robert, 42, 118
Pastan, Linda, 98
Petrakos, Chris, 113
Price, Nancy, 6
Rich, Adrienne, 5
Richman, Norma Hope, 58
Roberts, George, 9, 46
Roderick, John M., 34
Ruffin, Paul, 67
Rutsala, Vern, 70
Scheele, Roy, 136
Scott, Winfield Townley, 83
Shelton, Richard, 78, 146
Simpson, Mark, 101
Sklarew, Myra, 95

Smith, John, 96
Stafford, William, 72, 117, 124, 139
Steele, Frank, 68, 93, 139
Stetler, Charles B., 49
Strand, Mark, 86, 118
Sutter, Barton, 79
Swenson, May, 138
Teasdale, Sara, 103
Thomas, Rudy, 142
Tillinghast, Richard, 94
Treece, Henry, 146

Updike, John, 69
Valaitis, Laura, 141
Vinz, Mark, 91, 114
Wallace, Ronald, 14, 57, 64, 108
Wayne, Jane O., 114
Welch, Don, 18
Wilson, Keith, 88, 115
Worley, Jeff, 15
Wormser, Baron, 47
Young, Ree, 106
Zimmer, Paul, 82, 123, 140